Visual Identity

Susan Westcott Alessandri is a member of the communication and journalism faculty at Suffolk University. Prior to joining Suffolk University, Dr. Alessandri was on the faculty of the S.I. Newhouse School of Public Communications at Syracuse University.

Dr. Alessandri holds a PhD in mass communication from the University of North Carolina at Chapel Hill. Her research has been published in several books and journals, including *Corporate Reputation Review*, *Corporate Communications: An International Journal*, *Education Review of Business Communication*, *Journal of Marketing for Higher Education*, *Journal of Advertising Education*, and *Journal of Employee Communication Management*.

Visual Identity

Promoting and Protecting the Public Face of an Organization

Susan Westcott Alessandri

M.E.Sharpe
Armonk, New York
London, England

Library of Congress Cataloging-in-Publication Data

Alessandri, Susan Westcott.
  Visual identity : promoting and protecting the public face of an organization /
by Susan Westcott Alessandri.
       p. cm.
Includes bibliographical references and index.
ISBN 978-0-7656-2266-2 (cloth : alk. paper)—ISBN 978-0-7656-2267-9 (pbk. : alk. paper)
1. Organizational change. 2. Business enterprises. I. Title.

  HD58.8.A6774 2009
  659.2—dc22   2009006870

Printed in the United States of America

CW (c)	10	9	8	7	6	5	4	3	2	1
CW (p)	10	9	8	7	6	5	4	3	2	1

To Jackson Oleg Alessandri,
whose identity has *always* been clear,
strong, and consistent

Contents

Preface and Acknowledgments

Before embarking on my academic career, I worked for Lifeline Systems, a mid-size company that provided personal response services for the elderly and at-risk. We were constantly confused with our competitor, LifeCall, because of its irritatingly memorable advertising campaign: Mrs. Fletcher falling and yelling, "I've fallen, and I can't get up." The ad achieved cult-like status and became an oft-quoted and oft-parodied punchline in the national media.

As a rule, my company did not engage in national advertising; we worked with physicians and hospitals directly to put our product and service in the hands and homes of those who needed it most. This is one reason we were often confused with LifeCall: we had no national advertising presence. Instead of fighting the confusion head-on in an attempt to protect the company's brand name, Lifeline Systems took a tactical, ad hoc approach to educating the public about the company, stressing that we were the oldest, largest, and most well-respected player in the market. When competing against the cult-like "I've fallen, and I can't get up," tagline, however, our piecemeal approach to protection was a constant uphill climb.

When actress Dorothy McHugh, who played Mrs. Fletcher and uttered those fateful words, died in July 1995, the national media called Lifeline Systems for its reaction. Again, it was time to educate the media one reporter at a time. As of this writing, Dorothy McHugh's IMDb online profile still inaccurately states that she famously appeared in a commercial for Lifeline Systems.

It wasn't until I began researching visual identity issues during graduate school that I realized the extent of the marketing issue Lifeline was facing: trademark genericide. From a legal standpoint, the confusion with LifeCall and other personal response companies meant that Lifeline Systems was in danger of becoming the generic name of an entire product category. By not protecting our trademark through a massive educational effort, we were also in danger of losing the trademark. In putting a name to the phenomenon, I was able to begin to understand the complexities of visual identity and how it was at the core of product brands, companies, and organizations.

So what exactly is an organization's visual identity? Well, much like people, organizations have personalities, and all of what we know and think about their personality comes through in the organization's visual identity. Just as a person's name, appearance, clothing style, and behavior make up his or her identity, an organization's visual identity stems from its mission and manifests itself in the organization's behavior and the visual ways it presents itself: its name, logo, tagline, color palette, and even the architecture of the building in which it is housed.

Even though a visual identity helps form the organization's image, and ultimately its reputation, there are surprisingly few full-length books dedicated to the topic. In the books that do explore visual identity, the concept is almost always discussed only in the larger context of the organization's image or reputation. When I began teaching graduate seminars on visual identity, I was forced to cobble together a series of readings that would illuminate the concepts. I believed the market needed a book that provided a thorough introduction to visual identity and a discussion of the ways in which organizations of all sizes can nurture and protect their visual identities.

This book explores the promotion and protection of visual identity from an organizational brand perspective (corporate, nonprofit, etc.) rather than a product brand perspective. That is, this book is focused on the visual identity of Procter & Gamble rather than Tide laundry detergent. The book is divided into two major sections. Part 1 covers the promotion of visual identity, while Part 2 covers the protection of visual identity. Within each part are four chapters, each covering a discrete concept, from the basics of visual identity to the use of trademark and copyright laws to protect an organization's visual identity from infringement and misuse. Each chapter is followed by a short fictional case study specifically tailored to stimulate discussion about the chapter's major concepts.

First and foremost, this book is intended for use as a classroom text. In courses focused on visual identity or corporate graphic design, however, this book can be used effectively as a main text. In courses focused more generally on corporate communications, branding, public relations, or advertising, it can be used as a supplementary text to delineate the concept of visual identity and contextualize it within the larger area of study.

While this book is intended for classroom use, I also believe it can be useful for organizations hoping to better understand visual identity. Many organizations—particularly smaller ones with limited budgets—might use this book a reference during the development of a new identity, or as a guide in protecting their identities. In any event, regardless of how it is used, I hope it is as useful to read as it was enjoyable to write.

Acknowledgments

Thank you to Harry Briggs and Elizabeth Granda of M.E. Sharpe. Harry kept this project on track even through my move to a new city and a new school. Elizabeth provided invaluable technical advice to aid in the preparation of the manuscript.

Several colleagues reviewed chapters at the end of their own busy semesters. I owe them a debt of gratitude: Jim O'Rourke of the Mendoza College of Business at the University of Notre Dame, Laura "Lolly" Gasaway at the University of North Carolina at Chapel Hill School of Law, and Victoria Smith Ekstrand at Bowling Green State University. They provided invaluable feedback and helped make this work stronger. Any mistakes in this book are purely my own. Thank you, too, to Stan Wakefield, who made me believe there is no such thing as a random e-mail.

I would also like to thank my parents, Lois and Bill Westcott, and siblings Kelli, Bill, and Matt for their encouragement and support. Few families have a more diverse collection of individual identities that all seem to so work well together.

And finally, thank you to Todd for always understanding—both me and my minor obsession with all things visual identity.

Susan Westcott Alessandri
Boston

Part 1

Promotion of Visual Identity

1

Introduction to Basic Concepts

What Is Visual Identity?

Brands and organizations of all kinds (any public or private corporation, nonprofit, nongovernmental organization, school, or team) have personalities, and most of what we know about these organizations comes through in what we see or hear—or smell—about them. All of these things—what we see, hear, or even smell—make up a concept known as visual identity.

> In order to understand, develop, and manage its identity, the leaders of an organization must first understand those elements that combine to make up an identity. Next, they must set up a structure that will allow for the development of the identity they want to project. Finally, they must use that structure to monitor and manage that identity. This enables leaders of an organization to harness its identity and use it as a resource. In short, every organization has an identity. Either the organization can control its identity, or the identity will control the organization. (Olins and Selame 1993)

Many consumer packaged-goods (CPG) companies instinctively understand the power of having a strong visual identity. In 1890, Aunt Jemima was brought to life by R.T. Davis, the new owner of a self-rising pancake flour company. He hired former slave Nancy Green to act as spokesperson for the brand. It was not until the early 1930s, however, that the now-famous Aunt Jemima icon began to represent the brand in a larger way. Anna Robinson, described as "a large, gregarious woman with the face of an angel," made her debut at the 1933 Chicago World's Fair. She was the official Aunt Jemima until her death in 1951 (www.auntjemima. com). Aunt Jemima's fame grew; the company trademarked the image in 1937 and began advertising on television during the 1950s. Given the nature of the Aunt Jemima trademark, and the fact that she derives from a vaudeville act done in blackface, the Quaker Oats company has updated the look of Aunt Jemima on product packaging to reflect a more modern woman. In 1989, Aunt Jemima lost her headscarf and started wearing pearl earrings and a lace collar. Today, according to the company, "Aunt Jemima products continue to stand for warmth, nourishment and trust" (www.auntjemima.com).

Organization Defined

Consumer packaged-goods companies may have the most visible of visual identities, since the public is used to seeing these identities in a variety of media, but organizations of all sizes, types, and levels notoriety have visual identities. In this book, an organization is defined quite broadly:

> In an organization there is a sense of interdependence among members who occupy positions in a hierarchy and attempt to achieve common goals. A hierarchy may be quite informal, but there is always some division of labor and some sense of who makes the final decisions. (DeWine 2001, p. 6)

Given this broad definition of an organization, it is easy to see that businesses of all kinds are considered organizations, but also that nonprofits, schools, colleges and universities, and even ad hoc neighborhood groups are considered organizations. In each one of these cases, the organization must pay close attention to its visual identity, for it has one even if it does not consciously work to project it.

Visual Identity Defined

The concept of identity is studied in many different fields and from many perspectives. The concept of *visual identity*, however, is quite distinct, and is a concept most closely aligned with the marketing and communications disciplines. In some cases, visual identity is studied in the management area, since the overall identity of an organization is a strategic function. This is a compelling point, since the importance of visual identity needs to be understood throughout the organization as a component of the organization's success.

> The importance and potential role of an identity management system can be best described by comparing it to other systems already functioning in the organization. Perhaps the two most significant and appropriate role

models to help people throughout the organization think about identity management are financial management and information technology management, both of which are accepted as standard resources in successful institutions. (Olins and Selame 1993)

The concept of visual identity is defined in this book as a strategically planned and purposeful presentation in order to gain a positive organizational image in the minds of the public. A positive identity is established in order to gain a favorable reputation over time. More practically speaking, an organization's visual identity includes all of the observable and measurable elements of the organization's identity manifest in its comprehensive visual presentation of itself, including—but not limited to—its name, logo, tagline, color palette, and architecture. Visual identity also includes the organization's public behavior, including—but not limited to—its reception of employees, customers, shareholders, and suppliers.

In relating this once again to personality, there is a parallel between an organization's visual identity and a person's identity. An organization's name, logo, tagline, color palette, architecture, and behavior make up its visual identity, and a person's name, appearance, clothing style, and behavior make up his or her identity.

In defining the concept of branding, the American Marketing Association actually delineates the nuances of an organization's visual identity:

> A brand is the feel of your business card, the way the company's phone is answered, the tone of a letter, the package that's almost impossible to open, the receptionist at the corporate office who continues to chat with a fellow worker when a customer arrives, the instructions that are too hard to follow, the lane-hogging driver of a corporation's truck. The brand is every touch point and every thought the customer has about the brand. (Promotional Products Association International brochure)

Identity → Image

An organization's identity is a set of individual elements, or components, that make up a part of its marketing toolkit. Taken as a whole, however, these elements make up the persona of the firm, or its gestalt, so strategy must play a role in the development of an identity. Most organizations are savvy enough to know that identity is a strategic issue, since they

Figure 1.1   **A Model of Organizational Visual Identity**

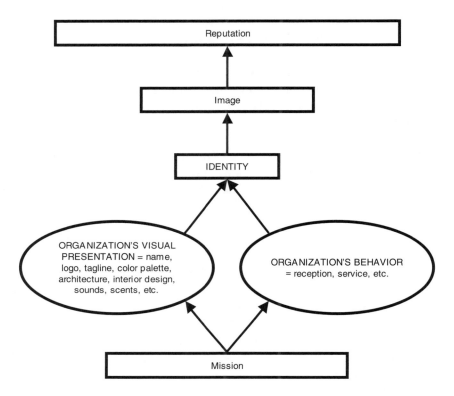

realize that how the organization looks and acts affects what the public thinks of it.

The model of organizational visual identity presented in Figure 1.1 illustrates the process by which an organization's visual identity affects the public's perception (the image) of the organization. In this model, the organizational mission is synonymous with the firm's philosophy (Abratt 1989; Leuthesser and Kohli 1997). The assumption is that every firm has a mission, whether tacit or codified, and that this mission is personified through the visual presentation of the organization as well as its behavior—the two complementary parts that make up the organizational visual identity. These components of the identity are within the organization's control (Lambert 1989; Leitch 1999; Topalian 1984) and may be manipulated or altered at the organization's discretion.

While the organization can—and should—control how it projects its identity, it is unable to control how that identity is perceived. This perception refers to the organization's *image*, which results from people's associations with the identity as a result of their interactions or experiences with it (Gray and Balmer 1998; Gregory and Wiechmann 1999; Topalian 1984).

An organization's image typically results from two types of associations—those that are inherent and those that are built over time. For example, Prudential uses a stylized drawing of the Rock of Gibraltar as its logo. The rock's inherent associations are with longevity and strength, two qualities that any insurance and financial services company would want associated with their firm. An example of a logo whose associations were built over time is the Nike Swoosh. Legend has it that Phil Knight, the founder of Nike, asked his graphic designer for a logo that connoted speed and motion. Because the Swoosh is a fabricated design, there is no way for it to have inherent associations: these are built over time and according to how that identity is projected and promoted.

This distinction between identity and image is integral to understanding how to maximize the effects of a visual identity. Since organizations retain complete control of their identities, but have no control over their image (Bronson 1985; Leitch 1999; Margulies 1977; Topalian 1984), the best way for an organization to cultivate what the public thinks of it is to *indirectly* control its image by *directly* controlling its identity. This is possible through interpersonal contact with stakeholders, but the most widespread exposure is likely to occur through formal marketing and mass communications channels, since most consumers lack a personal relationship with the organization.

Identity + Image = Reputation

Research indicates that the root of a brand or organization's reputation is in its identity. A consistent visual identity delivered through an organization's coordinated communications and public behavior can produce a positive image in the minds of an organization's stakeholders. Over time, repeated exposure to an organization's image serves to produce a positive reputation (Bronson 1985; Gray and Balmer 1998; Gregory and Wiechmann 1999; Markwick and Fill 1997; van Riel 1997).

The model presented here reflects the relationship among these three constructs (identity, image, and reputation) as a bottom-up process: the mission affects identity, identity affects image, and image builds the reputation over time. The reputation is less fleeting than an image, and is formed over time through the overall impressions of the image. As a result, an organization's investment in its visual identity could ultimately pay off in the form of a positive reputation.

The theoretical underpinning of the relationship among the constructs of identity, image, and reputation is rooted in the psychological literature. It assumes that a "learning" of perceptions works in two stages: at a low-involvement level and, after an image has been formed, through classical conditioning.

The scholarly study of visual identity is relatively new, but as early as 1942, the U.S. Supreme Court recognized the commercial—and psychological—nature of symbols. Justice Felix Frankfurter (1942) wrote:

> The protection of trade-marks is the law's recognition of the psychological function of symbols. If it is true that we live by symbols, it is no less true that we purchase goods by them. A trade-mark is a merchandising short-cut which induces a purchaser to select what he wants, or what he has been led to believe he wants.

Frankfurter's recognition that symbolism is most successful if it is widely recognized and known supports the theoretical explanation asserted here, that the public must first recognize the identity and then be conditioned to form a positive image of the identity.

Low Involvement

While there are several theories of consumer behavior that explain the ways in which consumers make purchase decisions (Rotzoll and Haefner 1996), the theory of low involvement is most useful for explaining how a consumer may actually come to recognize an organization's identity. Krugman (1965) developed the theory of low involvement, for the first time asserting that a behavioral trigger may activate an awareness generated through repetition of a message. This behavior may then result in attitude change. Krugman describes the process of attitude change through low involvement this way: repetition of a message will bring about a two-step process in which repetition will move some information from short-term to long-term memory, and a change in the perception of the brand will occur (Krugman 1965). Based on the theory of low involvement, communicators may be optimistic that each of their messages is reaching the audience on some level (Heath 1999).

The views on identity of Melewar and Saunders (2000) reinforce the notion that a type of low-involvement learning results from the repetition of the elements of a visual identity. They advocate projecting a consistent visual identity, which is integral to forming a positive image through classical conditioning, the second phase of the "learning" of an identity.

Classical Conditioning

Identity consultant Clive Chajet once remarked to a reporter, "A name is an abstract tool. You make it what it is" (Townsend 1990). Chajet's theory of attaching psychological meanings to words is an example of classical conditioning, when the public forms an attitude—in effect, learns a behavior—based on associations (Eagly and Chaiken 1993, p. 393). The theory of classical conditioning asserts that systematically pairing a conditioned stimulus with an unconditioned stimulus over time will produce a particular emotion or attitude, the conditioned response. In the case of visual identity, the conditioned stimulus would be the elements of the identity itself. The unconditioned stimulus would be the association—either positive or negative—paired with those elements. After repeated pairings of the stimuli, the result—the conditioned response—would be a favorable attitude toward the organization when viewing its logo or hearing its name.

Using classical conditioning in a marketing context is not new (Allen and Shimp 1990; Grossman and Till 1998; Janiszewski and Warloop 1993), since the ultimate goal of communicating a brand's attributes has always been the transfer of positive associations (Severin and Tankard 1992). The theory of classical conditioning has an interesting connection to visual identity, however, since the word "identity" comes from the Latin *identi dem*, which means "repeatedly," or "the same each time" (Balmer 1997).

Discussion of Identity Elements

An organization may choose to communicate one or more of its visual identity elements across any number of media. The most common visual identity elements are described and explained below.

Name

An organization or brand's name is its primary form of identification—
the element that is referenced by consumers and typically communicated
both visually and aurally in communications. As a result, an appropriate
name is one that is well thought out and one that results from strategic
thinking about the organization or brand.

Schmitt and Simonson (1997) believe there are specific characteristics that make up effective corporate and brand names. They are short
and memorable, the name says something about the product and its
key benefits, the name should be easy to pronounce and write, and the
name should be usable worldwide. This last characteristic is especially
important for two related reasons: the rise and growth of online communication and the global nature of business. In order for an organization's name to be effective in today's business environment, it must
effectively transcend language and connotation. That is, it must have
ability to be translated into numerous languages while also retaining
its meeting.

The characteristics articulated by Schmitt and Simonson (1997) are
reflected in the names chosen for organizations, whether they are for-
profit firms or nonprofit organizations. Generally, organizational names
fit into one of several categories: founder, descriptive, fabricated, metaphor, and acronym.

Founder

Naming an organization after its founder is popular with several types
of organizations, among them law firms and advertising agencies. This
naming strategy helps to fuel the perception that there is a certain level of
accountability on the part of the organization's leaders, since we "know"
them. Other organizations may choose to use only part of the founder's
name, as is the case with Dell Computer.

This strategy also includes using the names of those close to the organization's leaders or owners—Mercedes and Wendy's are both brands
named for the daughters of their founders—or a combination of parts
of the founder's name. For example, Adidas was named for its founder,
Adolf Dassler, but the name represents his nickname, Adi, and the first
three letters of his last name (www.adidas.com).

Descriptive

A descriptive name describes what the organization is or does. This type of strategy was very popular during the late 1990s and into the year 2000 with the proliferation of dot-com companies that needed to get their messages out quickly. The online company names of pets.com, drugstore. com, and stamps.com all gave Internet users a very good idea of what the sites sold. Not all descriptive names are so basic, however. Toys "R" Us is a descriptive name for a toy store that is also somewhat creative.

Fabricated

Fabricated names are made up for the specific purpose of serving as a brand name. For example, Kodak, Xerox, and Häagen-Dazs are all words that never existed—until they were developed as brand names. Newer examples include telecommunications giant Verizon and Altria, the parent company of Philip Morris International. The Verizon name resulted from the combination of "vertical" and "horizon" (www.brandingstrategy.org). In the context of telecommunications, this name brings about positive connotations, since it implies a 360-degree perspective. This is fitting in a wireless world.

Altria illustrates another trend in fabricated names: organizations look at word origin for inspiration, but then adapt the name to their specific uses. According to the company (formerly Philip Morris), Altria is derived from the Latin *altus*, which "conveys the notion of 'reaching ever higher'" (www.altria.com).

Metaphor

Metaphoric names are actual words that organizations co-opt for their own purposes. Nike, for example, is the name of the Greek Goddess of Victory. Sprint connotes speed. Amazon.com conveys an image of size, which customers will assume means the Web site will sell whatever it is they are looking to buy.

Acronym

Organizational names are often too long to be convenient, so the names are shortened into acronyms. The most famous of these examples include

International Business Machines (IBM), Cable News Network (CNN), and Minnesota Mining and Manufacturing (3M). In other cases, the acronym itself is the intended brand name, but there needs to be a meaning behind it, as in the case of DKNY (Donna Karan New York) or FCUK (French Connection United Kingdom).

Another type of acronym name began to appear during the technology boom: companies in the high-tech industry began to adopt brand names that begin with a lowercase "e" to further the perception that the organization was "electronic" (as in eHarmony or eBay). Another trend in the technology industry is to use "i" in brand or organizational names to reflect their "Internet" nature. As the Apple iPod, iPhone, and i-line of products grow, however, this one letter becomes more closely and specifically associated with Apple Computer, Inc., potentially leaving other organizations with the need to develop a new acronym.

Promotion Strategy

Regardless of the type of name an organization chooses, it must be promoted in order to generate awareness. Depending on its size and complexity, the organization has a choice to make in terms of promotion strategy for its visual identity. Aaker and Joachimsthaler (2000) define promotion strategy as the "organizing structure of the brand portfolio that specifies the brand roles and the relationships among brand and different product-market brand contexts" (p. 134). Simply put, the promotion strategy defines the way the organization chooses to publicly promote the relationship between itself and any product brands it may sell.

Wally Olins (1990), an identity strategist and the founder of a well-known identity consultancy, has identified three brand promotion strategies from which to choose: the monolithic strategy, the endorsed strategy, and the branded strategy. While not all organizations or brands will fit neatly into one of these categories, viewing these strategies as part of a continuum (see Figure 1.2) can help marketers choose the promotion strategy that best suits their own naming promotion needs. Olins differentiates and defines the strategies as follows:

A *monolithic* strategy refers to the decision to employ a stand-alone organizational brand, such as Reebok or Microsoft, as opposed to employing a branding approach that highlights individual product brands. Olins (1990) writes that a monolithic branding strategy provides firms with the strength of consistency across media and brands, since employ-

Figure 1.2   **The Visual Identity Promotion Strategy Continuum**

Monolithic ─────────▶ Endorsed ─────────▶ Branded

Organizational name   Combination of organizational   Product brand names
                             and product brand names

ing the organization's name as the product brand name means that every promotional activity supports all the others (Keller 1999).

An *endorsed* strategy employs the organizational brand name alongside an individual product brand name, such as IMB ThinkPad. By employing an endorsed branding strategy, organizations are able to draw on the associations linked to the overall organizational identity in order to build higher-order associations in the minds of the public (Keller 1999).

A *branded* strategy refers to foregoing the use of an organizational name on brands and other communications with the public (through advertising, public relations, etc.) in exchange for individual product or service brands. In the consumer packaged-goods (CPG) context, this strategy is referred to as the "P&G approach" (referring to Procter & Gamble): the company brands its individual products (e.g., Crest toothpaste or Tide laundry detergent) without the Procter & Gamble name.

Naming Decisions

In addition to new ventures or start-up organizations, which obviously need names, mergers and acquisitions also present strategic naming opportunities. Balmer and Dinnie (1999) interviewed senior managers and consultants involved in mergers across several industries and found that questions of corporate identity and corporate communications might be key factors in the success or failure of a merger.

While developing the name of an organization might seem like an easy decision to make, and one that can be made quickly, what a lot of organizations underestimate is the emotional attachment many organizations have to their names—or the prestige that accompanies one or both of the names involved in a merger. For this reason, the naming decision is very difficult, and one that can become emotionally charged. Often, under these circumstances, an awkward name results from both sides wanting to be sure their legacy organizations are represented. This is the case with a well-known and highly respected New York hospital. On the hospi-

Table 1.1

Examples of Merger-related Naming Strategies

Naming Strategy	Merging Organizations	New Name
Either existing Name	SBC & AT&T	AT&T
Combination of both names	Sirius & XM (satellite radio)	Sirius XM Radio
New name	Bell Atlantic & GTE	Verizon

tal's Web site, the banner identifies it as "New York–Presbyterian: The University Hospital of Columbia and Cornell." In press releases on the site, the hospital refers to itself differently—as "NewYork–Presbyterian Hospital/Weill Cornell Medical Center" (www.nyp.org). The first name contains twenty-four syllables, and the second has twenty-three. Neither is easy to say or remember. This naming reflects two organizations in the organization's new name, but the practical result nullifies the namers' intentions: consumers will shorten the very long name to something easier to say, such as "New York Presbyterian," or "New York Pres."

Organizations formed through a merger or acquisition typically have three choices when deciding on a name for the newly formed organization: one of the organization's existing names is chosen, the newly merged organization adopts both "legacy" names, or the new organization takes on an altogether new name (Gander 1999). Table 1.1 shows each of these strategies reflected in high-profile mergers.

Logo

A logo is the visual symbol that a brand or company uses to identify itself to consumers. Henderson and Cote (1998) define a logo as "the graphic design that a company uses, with or without its name, to identify itself or its products" (p. 14). In the context of this definition, a logo might be simply a stand-alone graphic element—an icon—like the Nike Swoosh or the Target Bullseye, or it can be a word designed in a special typeface. The latter is called a logotype; examples of companies that use a logotype as their primary means of identification include FedEx and jetBlue. When a logotype is employed, there is no additional visual, so the typeface chosen for the logotype is a strategic decision. The typeface must project the tone and style the organization is trying to achieve.

The decision to use a purely graphic or iconic logo or a simple logotype is dependent upon the image the organization would like to cultivate in the minds of the public, but in a study of what makes an effective logo, Henderson and Cote (1998) advocate developing a logo with a familiar meaning, as this improves recognition and consensus among those who view the logo. As with promoting any visual identity elements, however, the key to successfully exploiting either an iconic logo or a logotype is consistency in promotion.

Tagline

A tagline is the official name for the short phrase typically used in conjunction with a brand or organization's name or logo (e.g., GE: "imagination at work"). It is also referred to colloquially as a "motto" or "slogan." The word *slogan* is actually derived from the Scots word *sluagh-ghairm*, which referred to the war cries used by Scottish clans in the sixteenth century.

Unlike an organization's name or even its logo, the tagline typically does not stand alone in marketing. It is a complementary identity element, and one that is changed more often than any other identity element. The tagline will change over time and on a number of different occasions: when there is a new creative campaign developed, or when a new advertising agency is hired, or simply when the tagline has outlived its usefulness.

Color Palette

In 1995, the Supreme Court provided marketers and identity consultants with a new legally protected way of projecting a brand when it ruled that color alone could be registered as a trademark (*Qualitex* 514 U.S. 159). While organizations have always used color as a part of their marketing mix, never before was there the opportunity to "own" a color, both figuratively and literally.

Since the nineteenth century, Coca-Cola has been marketing itself almost exclusively using the color red. As a result, Coke's number one competitor, Pepsi, decided in the early 1990s that it didn't "own" a color the way Coke owned red. The company did research and determined that blue was "modern and cool, exciting and dynamic, and a color that communicated refreshment" (Quelch 1998). Ryobi, the maker of power tools, is another organization that uses blue, in combination with yellow, as part of its signature color palette. This rather bright combination of colors is likely to make the brand stand out in the sea of grays and browns that dominate home improvement stores.

Organizations may use one or more colors (a palette) in their identities, but more and more organizations are building their identity promotion and strategies around a signature color. Tiffany, for example, has forged very strong associations with its robin's egg blue boxes with white ribbons, and UPS has personified itself in the color brown by asking, "What can brown do for you?" Finally, IBM, known colloquially as "Big Blue," built on that nickname for years during the technology boom by including blue color strips at the top and bottom of its television advertisements.

Architecture and Interior Design

If an organization wants to truly project its identity in every facet of its presentation, it has the ability to use architecture and interior design as elements of its identity. This is one way to ensure that the identity is diffused not just through communications, but also in person to customers and other stakeholders.

This type of identity projection makes sense in the context of how we think about different types of organizations: advertising agencies have a different look and feel than law firms and banks, and much of this is by design to reflect a certain ethos about the organization. Advertising agencies are selling creativity, while law firms and banks tend to want to project a more serious identity.

Viewing an organization's architecture or interior design as a reflection of its identity is not always cut-and-dried. The assumption is that organizations have consciously chosen the design of both their exteriors and interiors. In some cases, however, an organization's architectural and interior design elements may be by default: it is housed in a building not specifically designed for it; rather, it was available and met functional needs of the organization, rather than having the distinct design the organization would choose if given the opportunity.

An example of an organization that builds its identity into its architecture is Nike. Each of the buildings on its "campus" is named after one of its paid athletic endorsers: Michael Jordan, Mia Hamm, and

Lance Armstrong. In the building known as "The Lance" is a Tour de France simulator, a set of four bikes that, through virtual reality, allow cyclists to re-create portions of the Tour de France stages. In addition, the 60,000-square-foot building contains an 11-lane swimming pool, a children's pool, a 34-foot climbing wall, spinning studio, and a Pilates studio. Outside "The Lance" is a putting green made from more than 23,000 pairs of Nike sneakers ("Nike Names Building After Lance Armstrong" 2001).

Although it is not technically architecture, outside the L.L. Bean flagship store in Freeport, Maine, is an enormous boot statue. It is a replica of the now-famous hunting boot on which the company was founded. In addition to serving as a visual identity element, the boot statue has become an oft-visited symbol of the store—a tourist attraction that prides itself on never locking its doors because it is open 24 hours per day, 365 days per year.

Sounds

Employing sound as part of an identity strategy gives the organization's marketers a number of choices, from single sounds to jingles to entire songs. This type of strategy also allows an organization to use original sounds or songs as well as those produced for another purpose but co-opted by the organization for its own identity promotion.

One example of an organization that employs sound as part of its identity strategy is NBC. The so-called peacock network uses the musical notes G, E, and C to make up its "chimes" trademark, used in on-air promotion for its programming. While not elaborate, the composition is unique in that it instantly identifies NBC as the network airing the specific programming.

Another sound used to identify the source of a media organization is the trademarked lion's roar that can be heard at the beginning of movies produced by MGM. Harley-Davidson tried unsuccessfully for years to trademark the sound of its "common crankpin V-Twin engine," which the motorcycle maker believed was a unique identifier of its motorcycles (Sapherstein 1998).

While there are very few actual sound trademarks registered by the U.S. Patent and Trademark Office, there are many companies and brands that recognize that specific sounds can be efficient ancillary— and memorable—parts of their identities. Specifically, department and specialty retailers use music to set a tone for shoppers. Retailers such as Starbucks, Abercrombie & Fitch, Victoria's Secret, and Pottery Barn all sell musical CDs. The music contained on them is played in the retail stores, which both sets a tone and reflects the identity of the stores, and at the same time represents another profit motive for the organization.

Scents

Schmitt and Simonson (1997) write that the memory associated with scent is the strongest part of the human memory. Because it can be so powerful in terms of association building, and because there are a wide variety of scents to choose from, building an identity that incorporates scent is possible in a variety of situations where the customer has a personal interaction with the organization, as is the case with retailers.

Mascots

Some organizations use mascots to personify their brands. While this has most often been the purview of colleges and universities, pharmaceutical companies have adopted the practice in their direct-to-consumer (DTC) advertising. In fact, Mr. Mucus, the green blob that serves as the mascot for the Mucinex brand, is such an integral part of the brand's marketing that recent advertisements have depicted Mr. Mucus getting married and even having a child. This is all in an attempt to personify the brand, but also to help build associations with Mucinex that will cut through advertising clutter. Other examples of organizations that employ mascots as part of their identities include Aflac's use of a duck and GEICO's use of a gecko.

Summary

An organization's visual identity is reflected in how its presents itself to the public. This identity is made up of the organization's name, logo, tagline, color palette, architecture, interior design, sounds, scents, mascots, and its public behavior. People form associations with this identity, which forms an image. Over time, impressions of this image form the reputation, which is enduring.

Case Study: Developing a Visual Identity for Cakewalk Pastry

Susan Jacoby sat at her culinary school graduation, envisioning the grand opening of her new bakery, Cakewalk Pastry. Since it was a start-up venture, Susan knew there were still a lot of details to work out, but at least a site and financing—and a great name—were secured. Everything else was just busywork, Susan thought happily.

As the speaker continued to talk about the joys of a life in the culinary arts, Susan continued to run down the list of details that needed taking care of, including a sign for the bakery, a painter to paint the inside walls, and a design for the invitations to the bakery's grand opening. It occurred to Susan that the remaining details she needed to tend to all related to how she would present her bakery—how it would look to customers and the public generally. The more she thought about it, the more she began to think of these things as much more than "details" to be worked out: these decisions needed serious thought.

At home later that evening, culinary degree in hand, Susan sat down to make a list of the things she needed to decide on: the type of sign that would identify the bakery to passersby, the color of the inside of the bakery that would make customers the most comfortable as they sat and enjoyed their pastry, and a design for the grand opening party invitations. Again, Susan began to think about how all of these marketing decisions were interrelated, so her first task was to think about the elements that would make up the sign and the interior design, since those would influence how the invitations looked.

She tried to put herself in the shoes of her potential customers. If they were walking down the street and saw Cakewalk Pastry, what would they want to see? She wanted her customers to know that Cakewalk Pastry's products were fresh, delicious, and beautiful to look at. Somehow, Susan thought, she needed to reflect those values in her signage, her color scheme, and any printed material distributed on behalf of the bakery.

Case Discussion Questions

1. Susan Jacoby knows she needs to make some decisions regarding Cakewalk Pastry's visual identity—the "look and feel" it projects to customers. She'd like her customers and potential customers to think that her products are fresh, delicious, and beautiful. How can she reflect those values in Cakewalk Pastry's visual identity?

2. Susan already knows that Cakewalk Pastry needs a storefront sign, an interior paint color, and a printed invitation for the grand opening. What other visual identity elements does Susan need to consider before moving forward with the sign and the invitation?

3. A bakery is quite different from a multinational company or a non-profit organization. Are there additional visual identity elements that should come into play given this unique organization?

Bibliography

Aaker, D.A., and E. Joachimsthaler, 2000. *Brand Leadership*. New York, NY: Free Press.

Abratt, R. 1989. "A New Approach to the Corporate Image Management Process." *Journal of Marketing Management* 5, no. 1: 63–76.

Allen, C.T., and T.A. Shimp. 1990. "On Using Classical Conditioning Methods for Researching the Impact of Ad-evoked Feelings." In *Emotion in Advertising: Theoretical and Practical Exploration*, ed. S.J. Agres, J.A. Edell, and T.M. Dubitsky. Westport, CT: Quorum Books.

Balmer, J. M. T. 1997. "Corporate Identity: Past, Present and Future" (working paper). Glasgow: University of Strathclyde International Centre for Corporate Identity Studies.

Balmer, J.M.T., and Dinnie, K. 1999. "Merger Madness: The Final Coup de Grace." *Journal of General Management* 24, no. 4: 53–70.

Belson, K. 2006. "AT&T Bets Its Brand Is More Than Nostalgia." *New York Times*, July 21, p. 7.

Branding Strategy Web site. www.brandingstrategy.org.

Bronson, G. 1985. "As Companies Gamble on Creating New Images." *U.S. News and World Report*, September 16, p. 76.

Case, D. 2002. "Book Serves Up the Life of Syracuse's 'Aunt Jemima.'" *Syracuse Post-Standard*, November 3, Available at: www.syracusethenandnow.org/History/AuntJemima.htm. Accessed April 15, 2009.

DeWine, S. 2001. *The Consultant's Craft: Improving Organizational Communication*. 2nd ed. Boston: Bedford/St. Martin's.

Eagly, A.H., and S. Chaiken. 1993. *The Psychology of Attitudes*. Orlando, FL: Harcourt Brace College Publishers.

Frankfurter, F. 1942. U.S. Supreme Court. *Mishawaka Rubber and Woolen Manufacturing Co. v. S.S. Kresge Co.* Washington, DC: U.S. LEXIS 1224.

Gander, P. 1999. "Moniker Mayhem." *Marketing Week*, 41–43.

Gray, E.R., and J.M.T. Balmer. 1998. "Managing Corporate Image and Corporate Reputation." *Long Range Planning* 31, no. 5: 695–702.

Gregory, J.R., and J.W. Wiechmann. 1999. *Marketing Corporate Image: The Company as Your Number One Product*. Chicago: NTC Business Books.

Grossman, R.P., and B.D. Till. 1998. "The Persistence of Classically Conditioned Brand Attitudes." *Journal of Advertising* 27, no. 1: 23–31.

Hawn, R. 1998. "Image vs. Identity." *Trends* 14 (April/May): 22–27.

Heath, R. 1999. "'Just Popping Down to the Shops for a Packet of Image Statements': A New Theory of How Consumers Perceive Brands." *Journal of the Market Research Society* 41, no. 2: 153-169.

Henderson, P.W., and J.A. Cote. 1998. "Guidelines for Selecting or Modifying Logos." *Journal of Marketing* 62, no. 2: 14–30.

"How Many Names Can One Hospital Have?" 2006. *Rivkin and Associates: The Naming Newsletter.* Available at www.namingnewsletter.com. Accessed October 11, 2006.

Janiszewski, C., and L. Warloop. 1993. "The Influence of Classical Conditioning Procedures on Subsequent Attention to the Conditioned Brand." *Journal of Consumer Research* 20, no. 2: 171–189.

Keller, K.L. 1999. "Managing Brands for the Long Run: Brand Reinforcement and Revitalization Strategies." *California Management Review* 41, no. 3: 102–124.

Kern-Foxworth, M. 1990. "Ads Pose Dilemma for Black Women." Center for Media Literacy. Available at www.medialit.org/reading_room/article449.html. Accessed December 12, 2008.

Krugman, H.E. 1965. "The Impact of Television Advertising: Learning Without Involvement." *Public Opinion Quarterly* 29, no. 3: 349–356.

Lambert, A. 1989. "Corporate Identity and Facilities Management." *Facilities* 7, no. 12: 7–12.

Leitch, S. 1999. "From Logo-centrism to Corporate Branding?" *Australian Journal of Communication* 26, no. 3: 121.

Leuthesser, L., and C. Kohli. 1997. "Corporate Identity: The Role of Mission Statements." *Business Horizons* 40, no. 3: 59–66.

Margulies, W.P. 1977. "Make the Most of Your Corporate Identity." *Harvard Business Review*, July/August, pp. 66–74.

Markwick, N., and C. Fill. 1997. "Towards a Framework for Managing Corporate Identity." *European Journal of Marketing* 31, no. 5–6: 396–409.

Melewar, T.C., and J. Saunders. 2000. "Global Corporate Visual Identity Systems: Using an Extended Marketing Mix." *European Journal of Marketing* 34, no. 5/6: 538–550.

"Nike Names Building After Lance Armstrong." 2001. Available at www.totalbike. com/news/article/28/. Accessed January 3, 2008.

Olins, Wally. 1990. *The Wolff Olins Guide to Corporate Identity.* London: The Design Council.

Olins, W., and E. Selame. 1993. *The Corporate Identity Audit: A Set of Objective Measurement Tools for Your Company's Image and Reputation.* Switzerland: Strategic Direction Publishers Ltd.

Qualitex Company v. Jacobson Products Company, Inc., 514 U.S. 159 (1995).

Quelch, J.A. 1998. *Pepsi Blue.* Boston, MA: Harvard Business School.

Rotzoll, K.B., and J.E. Haefner. 1996. *Advertising in Contemporary Society: Perspectives Toward Understanding.* Urbana and Chicago: University of Illinois Press.

Sapherstein, M.B. 1998. "The Trademark Registrability of the Harley-Davidson Roar: A Multimedia Analysis." *Intellectual Property and Technology Forum.* Available at: www.bc.edu/bc_org/avp/law/st_org/iptf/articles/content/1998101101.html. Accessed January 8, 2008.

Schmitt, B.H., A. Simonson, and J. Marcus. 1995. "Managing Corporate Image and Identity." *Long Range Planning* 28, no. 5: 82–92.

Schmitt, B.H., and A. Simonson. 1997. *Marketing Aesthetics: The Strategic Management of Brands, Identity and Image.* New York: The Free Press.

Severin, W.J. & Tankard, J.W. 1992. *Communication Theories: Origins, Methods, and Uses in the Mass Media.* White Plains, NY: Longman Publishing Group.

Topalian, A. 1984. "Corporate Identity: Beyond the Visual Overstatements." *International Journal of Advertising* 3, no. 1: 55–62.

Townsend, B. 1990. "Cashing in on Corporate Identity." *American Demographics* 12 (July): 42–43.

van Riel, C.B.M. 1997. "Research in Corporate Communication: An Overview of an Emerging Field." *Management Communication Quarterly* 11, no. 2: 288–309.

2

Communicating a Visual Identity

Most people need to hear, see, or experience something more than once to truly understand it. For example, when an ad appears on television, you might not see the entire spot the first time, or you may hear the spot while you are busy doing something else, so you don't actually see the ad. It could take a few exposures before you can actively process the message being delivered by the ad. Marketers generally understand that integration of messages is important, and in the context of promotional communications, the term "integrated" has become singularly aligned with Integrated Marketing Communications (IMC), which refers to the idea that a brand will communicate most effectively if it engages in a dialogue with the public and sends a unified message through multiple media. IMC was developed during the 1980s, but it was not until Schultz, Tannenbaum, and Lauterborn (1993) literally wrote the book on IMC that it became a mainstream concept, and one that continues to be debated today on a number of fronts (Schultz et al. 2007).

What Is IMC?

Although they don't provide a formal definition of the concept, Schultz, Tannenbaum, and Lauterborn (1993) describe IMC as:

> A new way of looking at the whole, where once we only saw parts such as advertising, public relations, sales promotion, purchasing, employee communications, and so forth. It's realigning communications to look at it the way the customer sees it. . . . It means eliciting a response, not just conducting a monologue. And it means being accountable for results, not just readership scores or day-after recall—delivering a return on investment, not just spending a budget. (p. xvii)

The authors propose that in an oversaturated marketplace, the only true differentiators are logistics or communication. While logistics may be organization-dependent and therefore difficult to change, communication is one area where any organization can tailor its approach. The promise of an IMC approach is that integrated communication, based on consumer needs, will separate one organization from another by associating the organization with value in the minds of the public.

IMC Process

The revolutionary aspect of IMC is its focus on the public or, more specifically, the consumer. Traditional marketing works via the "push" method, which refers to an organization trying to reach consumers by simply pushing its product through a distribution chain. This strategy does not focus on what the consumer or end-user desires, but what the organization wants to give them—on its own terms. The IMC approach, conversely, is rooted in a pull strategy, whereby consumers are in control. These consumers use their buying influence to dictate what they pull through the distribution channel (Keller 1998).

This pull strategy depends upon a two-way model of communication that allows for dialogue between the organization and the public. The first step in developing a true IMC program is to start with the database. This is easier said than done for a lot of organizations, which may not have detailed information on their customers, donors, and so forth. Schultz et al. (1993) suggest that the minimum information needed for a database includes demographics, psychographics, and purchase or donation history. Other information should be added as it is collected.

The value of the database lies in its ability to be manipulated by the marketer to segment the market according to customer or prospect behavior. This differs from a traditional marketing approach since it segments users according to their past behavior rather than making assumptions about consumers' future intentions or present attitudes (Schultz et al. 1993).

After the database has been developed and the behaviors analyzed, the next step in an IMC program is to think about "contact management" (Schultz et al. 1993, p. 56). Far from the traditional marketing approach of disseminating widespread messages with the intention of reaching as much of the target audience as possible, contact management involves finding a time and a place that suits the target. The question of how and when has changed dramatically over the past decade, and consumers now have a growing and evolving range of communication options.

The third step in the IMC approach is to develop a communication strategy based on the contact management strategy. This refers to communicating in a creative way that suits the context under which the organization is trying to reach the customer or prospect. Along with the communication strategy, the organization must set a series of communication objectives for the IMC campaign, since it is only through measurable objectives that the organization will get an accurate view of how successful the campaign was.

Finally, once the database has been developed, the contact with the customer decided, and the strategy and objectives set, the organization needs to select the marketing tactics that will be used in the campaign. With the number of options for marketing communication growing with the proliferation of technology-based tools, the tactical vehicles available to marketers are unimaginable compared with those available just a decade ago.

The 4 Ps to the 4 Cs

In developing IMC as a concept, Schultz, Tannenbaum, and Lauterborn (1993) recognized the need to change the traditional marketing mindset of the four Ps (product, price, place, and promotion) to a more consumer-focused mindset. To add some structure to this change, the authors developed the four Cs: customer, cost, convenience, and communication. Figure 2.1 illustrates the change from the traditional marketing paradigm to the IMC approach. With a true IMC approach, the focus is the customer rather than the product, which reflects the importance of the database, but also the necessity of studying what the consumer wants rather than merely what the organization wishes to sell.

In a traditional marketing environment, the organization concerns itself with the price of its product, but in the IMC context the focus is turned around to concentrate on the cost of the product to the consumer. Put more simply, cost becomes figurative rather than just literal. Rather than just monetary price, the cost includes many intangible factors relevant to individual consumers. For example, consumers might not mind paying more for a product at a store close to their homes, since driving to a store farther away takes them away from their families for a longer period. The cost of being away from their families then becomes part of the cost of buying the product.

Related to cost is the convenience of buying a product. Whereas

Figure 2.1 **From the 4 Ps to the 4 Cs**

Product → Customer
Price → Cost
Place → Convenience
Promotion → Communication

once marketers were concerned only about getting products into stores, today organizations need to concern themselves with how and when a consumer can buy a product. It is probably unthinkable to some that it was once impossible to shop at a mall on a Sunday. Today consumers can shop any day of the week, but also in the middle of the night from the privacy of their own home computers.

Marketing has typically been about product or service promotion, a legacy of one-way communication directed at the target audience. With advances in technology and the realization that consumers are valuable, organizations have begun to focus on communication, a two-way model that stresses actual dialogue with consumers (Schultz et al. 1993).

IMC and Visual Identity

Because an organization's visual identity is at the core of its brand, and therefore its message, regardless of the strategy associated with *which* elements to promote, *how* the visual identity is promoted needs to be a strategic decision. In order to most effectively and efficiently promote the identity—and in turn the organization itself—an integrated approach is recommended. In fact, Markwick and Fill (1997) contend that the rise of IMC was one of a number of factors spurring increased interest in visual identity.

There are several reasons to advocate an IMC approach to promoting a visual identity, including the broadly accepted notion that repetition of campaign elements aids in the process of linking associations to an organization or brand (Aaker 1991; Aaker and Joachimsthaler 2000; Keller 1996; Lambert 1989). To ensure even more effective processing, Keller (1996) suggests using visual or verbal retrieval cues within integrated campaigns. In the case of visual identity, these visual or verbal cues may be the organization's name, logo, tagline, a color from its palette, or any of the sensory elements it actively tries to positively associate with itself.

Using visual or verbal cues from the visual identity supports what is known as the cue compatibility principle, which states that successful recall of communication effects from memory is most likely to occur when the type of information contained in the cues is compatible or congruent with the type of information already stored in memory (Keller 1996).

Message Consistency and Information Processing

An organization's visual identity requires message consistency to achieve positive associations, since it is only over time, through "learning" an identity, that people form associations. In order for the public to be fully exposed to the identity, it must be projected across media. The most efficient way to execute a truly consistent and integrated strategy is through IMC, where the assumption is that consumers and the general public tend to view all of a firm's communication as one indistinguishable flow of information (Schultz et al. 1993). The average consumer does not differentiate between the various forms of communication such as advertising, public relations, promotions, and so on. In addition, thinking about theories of information processing in the context of advertising promotions has changed how organizations view the effectiveness of their messages.

Pioneers of IMC developed the concept based on how they believe consumers process the information they receive. Just as we learn by building on the knowledge we already have in memory, rather than starting from scratch each time, marketers now understand that information is not replaced but is combined with existing messages stored in memory. Also, organizations need to remember that consumers are receiving—and trying to process—not just the messages *they* create, but those that are being created by tens of thousands of other organizations.

Given the reality of how people learn, a more credible model of information processing, the accumulation model, asserts that information is not replaced but is combined with existing messages stored in memory. This means that everything consumers see, hear, smell, and experience about an organization is stored away in memory for later retrieval. The theory behind this model of information processing has serious implications for organizations: it is not a matter of simply replacing existing messages, such as replacing a negative one with a positive one. It is a matter of developing and delivering a core message, and then developing communications that resonate with the public in the proper context.

A classic example of a company with a core message that resonated with consumers because of the way the company handled a crisis is Johnson & Johnson. In late 1982, seven people in Chicago died after taking Extra-Strength Tylenol capsules laced with cyanide. As a result, Johnson & Johnson voluntarily recalled all capsules nationwide, repackaged the product using tamper-resistant bottles, advertised to consumers in 184 newspapers nationally, and offered free product to consumers via newspaper coupons during two consecutive weeks—all at a cost of approximately $100 million to the company (Fannin 1983; Siomkos 1992). Because human life was at stake, but also because Johnson & Johnson understood the value of its organizational brand name and the trust its customers put in that name, the company undertook these efforts. By February, Johnson & Johnson had regained 65 percent of its Tylenol sales. Before the crisis, Tylenol's market share was 35 percent; by February, it was 24 percent. This seems alarming until you realize that marketing experts had said Johnson & Johnson would never be able to sell pain reliever again under the Tylenol brand name (Fannin 1983).

Using the accumulation model as a framework within the context of the Tylenol crisis, it is easy to understand why it is a valuable information-processing theory. In the case of Tylenol, consumers were able to draw on the trust they had in Johnson & Johnson and Tylenol, built up over years of experience with the company's positive reputation, the product, and its brand promotion. The bottom line with respect to the accumulation model suggests that those who send nonintegrated messages may risk not having their messages processed sufficiently to allow proper recall (Schultz, Tannenbaum, and Lauterborn 1993).

Criticism of IMC

For many years, critics of IMC have contended that IMC is not a valuable—or even workable—concept. Cornelissen and Lock (2000), for example, argue that IMC is more "management fashion" than theory. They cite a handful of reasons, including the fact that it is novel and oversimplified, and therefore not academically rigorous, and because managers employ IMC because it is the "rational norm," or because everyone else is doing it.

Cornelissen and Lock (2000) cite a viable criticism of IMC, specifically that Schultz et al. (1993) neglect to provide a definition of IMC. As a result, they argue, researchers are left without constructs to operationalize, test, and measure.

In response to Cornelissen and Lock (2000), Schultz and Kitchen (2000) contend that IMC was never conceived of as a theory, but as an evolutionary concept that is evolving along with the research being conducted on it. The authors refute the idea that IMC is just a management fashion simply because Cornelissen and Lock (2000) believe it is difficult to measure.

More recently, and even after more than a decade of widespread awareness of the concept, Schultz et al. (2007) recognize that IMC is a misunderstood concept, and one that is understudied in any rigorous or theoretical way. They also provide what had been missing all along: a definition of what IMC is. They write:

> Integration, in its simplest form, is the development, organization, alignment and implementation of [content, delivery systems, and audience or customers]. It is how the elements are coordinated and aligned that really make Integrated Marketing Communication. (p. 29)

Schultz et al. (2007) sought to find a "clearer definition and delineation view of IMC" by studying course syllabi to explore how and what colleges and universities around the world were teaching about the concept. Instead of finding a theoretical base for IMC among the syllabi, however, the authors found that IMC is often taught from a tactical perspective, and not from the strategic and integrative view Schultz and the IMC developers envisioned. To clarify the purpose and promise of IMC, Schultz et al. (2007) recognize that the three components to be integrated—content, delivery systems, and audience or customers—are not always equal. Rather, in some cases the audience or customer will be most important, and in others it might be the actual media (delivery system) used, or even the content of the message in some cases.

> The value of IMC, which has often been so difficult for both practitioners and academics to articulate, comes from the synergy created by the three elements when they are properly combined. That is, when the three ele-

ments are properly aligned and used in the proper manner, the marketplace effect is greater than when each is used separately or individually in the development of a communication program. (p. 29)

IMC and Media Tactics

In terms of marketing and media tactics, organizations today have a number of choices related to how to communicate a visual identity to consumers or to the public. Each of these choices is a "consumer touch-point," an opportunity to communicate a specific message and reinforce the identity.

Melewar (2001) introduced an international identity scale that delineates some of the major marketing and media choices available, many of them endorsed by other identity scholars. These choices include product packaging, building interiors/exteriors (Gray 1986; Olson, Cooper and Slater 1998; White 1992), signage, clothing (Pratt and Rafaeli 1997), stationery, forms, publications, vehicles, advertising, and promotions/give-away items. In addition to these choices, however, there are other specific options that may be effective in promoting an organization's identity, including public relations, organizational Web sites (Schmitt and Simonson 1997), and event sponsorship

What follows is a brief discussion of several of the major visual identity touchpoints mentioned above, as well as additional choices available to organizations for visual identity promotion.

Advertising

There are as many definitions of advertising in use by the academy and the profession as there are advertising professors and professionals (Richards and Curran 2002). While there are a variety of different definitions available, they generally have a few elements in common: advertising is paid, nonpersonal, has an identified sponsor, is disseminated through the mass media, and it is intended to persuade or influence.

Although these elements indeed describe most of what we consider traditional advertising, such as through magazines, television, or radio, these elements do not account for the many emerging "advertising" media, including social media Web sites and mobile phones. Nor do they accurately describe most outdoor advertising, including billboards, transit advertising, and bus shelters, since these are not mass media.

Richards and Curran (2002) offer an updated definition of advertising based on the responses from researchers and professionals. They write: "Advertising is a paid, mediated form of communication from an identifiable source, designed to persuade the receiver to take some action, now or in the future." This definition more accurately reflects the many varied media types now available, and it does not assume that an advertising message must be delivered through a mass medium. Perhaps most importantly, this definition helps to account for some of the latent effects of advertising, such as when a consumer sees an advertisement today but does not act until tomorrow—or even later.

Public Relations

Public relations is a strategy used by an organization's management to communicate with stakeholders. Cutlip, Center, and Broom (1994) define public relations as "the management function that establishes and maintains mutually beneficial relationships between an organization and the publics on whom its success or failure depends" (p. 1).

When employing a public relations strategy, there are a number of tactics to consider: press release templates and press kits, events, speeches, and both Web and paper publications, including annual and quarterly reports, newsletters, and backgrounders (a boilerplate summary of general information related to the organization).

Product Packaging

Meyers and Lubliner (1998) define a package as "any container intended to hold, protect, transport, store and identify a product" (p. 263). If the organization promoting its identity produces a consumer packaged good (CPG), the organization has the opportunity to communicate with customers from the store shelves. For this reason, product packaging has long been referred to as the "silent salesman."

Business-to-business organizations also have the opportunity to incorporate elements of their visual identities into packaging. For example, every cardboard box and packing material contained inside presents an opportunity to communicate with a customer or vendor.

Generally speaking, there are several questions to consider when developing packaging. For example, Meyers and Lubliner (1998) discuss package structure, package form, and package graphics. Package structure refers to "the shape, material, and functional components of a package," whereas package form is more basic and refers to "the type or shape of a package." Finally, they define package graphics as "the visuals that decorate the surface of a package and provide information about its contents."

Building Interiors and Exteriors

An organization's visual identity might include its building architecture and interior design, but there is also the opportunity to use the interior and exterior as promotional vehicles. For example, the company's name or logo—or any element of its identity—might be displayed on the inside or outside of its headquarters, sales offices, or retail stores. The same interiors might also be painted using a color from the organization's palette.

Signage

An organization often has signage both inside and outside its property. Every sign is an opportunity to reflect one or more elements of the organization's identity. Interior signage reminds current employees and other stakeholders of the presence of the identity and is another opportunity for the organization to reinforce positive associations. Exterior signage can also help to reinforce positive associations, but it is an additional opportunity to educate the public about the existence of the organization while projecting the visual identity elements.

Clothing

Clothing can be a used as a tactic in an organization's visual identity strategy in one of two ways: by requiring a dress code or official uniforms that are designed specifically with the identity in mind, or by making available to the public a set of identity-inspired clothing, such as logo shirts or other items incorporating one or more identity elements. Incorporating identity elements into an organization's uniforms or other clothing is a consistent and continuous way of reflecting the organizational identity.

Stationery and Forms

An organization's stationery products are staples in its marketing portfolio, since every organization, regardless of size, typically has the following: letterhead, envelopes, mailing labels, business cards, and checks. The point of letterhead is to identify the organization, so it is at the heart of projecting the visual identity. The other stationery items are additional tools in the identity arsenal and should be deployed at every available and appropriate opportunity.

Forms are another way that most organizations can reinforce their visual identities. Each time an organization sends a check to a vendor, or issues an invoice, there is the opportunity for elements of the organization's visual identity to be projected and reinforced.

Vehicles

If an organization is large enough to maintain a vehicle or a fleet of vehicles—whether cars, vans, buses, trains, or planes—using those vehicles is a tremendous opportunity to project the visual identity. Each time the vehicle is on the road, the visual identity is projected for every other driver to see.

In some cases, organizations use vehicles specifically as promotional tools rather than for their more functional purposes. The Goodyear blimps, for example, began flying in 1925 as "very visible corporate symbols" and "aerial ambassadors" for the company. Over time, Goodyear began mass-producing airships for the U.S. Navy, but today operates just three (www.goodyearblimp.com). Most associations people have with the Goodyear Blimp are likely linked with sporting events, where the blimps provide aerial coverage for the television network covering the event while at the same time garnering very expensive publicity—for free—for Goodyear.

Sales Promotion

Sales promotion is aimed at the short-term sales of products to consumers. Burnett and Moriarty (1998) define it as "marketing activities that add to the basic value of the product or service for a limited time and directly stimulate consumer purchasing, the cooperation of distributors, or the effort of the sales force." This type of tactic includes a wide variety of things, including coupons, BOGO (buy one, get one) offers, and all point-of-purchase (POP) displays. One study of promotional products by Promotional Products Association International found that consumers who have received a company's promotional product have a significantly more positive image of the company than those who did not receive any promotional products.

Sales promotion occurs on both the consumer and the trade level. Consumer promotions are offers developed for the retail consumer, but trade promotions are directed at resellers or sales forces. Either type of promotion provides an opportunity to reinforce one or more elements of the visual identity.

Brand Placement

In the 1982 blockbuster hit *E.T.*, a character named Elliot used a prominently displayed bag of Reese's Pieces to lure a friendly alien named E.T. out of his hiding place. When press reports indicated that the Hershey Company, maker of Reese's Pieces, realized a 65 percent increase in sales of the candy after the release of the film, the practice of using real branded products as props in films and television shows began to garner widespread attention (Balasubramanian, Karrh, and Patwardhan 2006). It also became a mainstream way of promoting a brand without it seeming as if the brand was being promoted.

Balasubramanian (1994) refers to this practice as a "hybrid message," and more specifically, as brand placement. He defines brand placement as a "paid product message aimed at influencing movie (or television) audiences via the planned and unobtrusive entry of a branded product into a movie (or television program)."

Brands have been used in films since the beginning of filmmaking itself, but *E.T.* helped organizations realize that they could profit from their brands' on-set participation in films and on television. In the ensuing decades, brand placement has become a semistructured promotional method with three general types of placements: organizations provide a brand for use on set in exchange for the free exposure, organizations pay a flat fee to the producer in order to have the brand show up in the film, or the organization and producer might have a formal arrangement that allows the organization to use promotional tie-ins with the film.

Although difficult to measure in terms of effectiveness, brand placements are perceived as effective because they are not discrete and explicit selling messages. In addition, brand placements are viewed as more organic than advertising because they produce positive associations for viewers between the brand and the film's protagonists.

Word of Mouth and Buzz

According to the Word of Mouth Marketing Association (WOMMA), word of mouth is "the act of consumers providing information to other consumers." Word of mouth becomes valuable to organizations when it turns into wordof-mouth marketing, which WOMMA defines as "giving people a reason to talk about your products and services, and making it easier for that conversation to take place" (Word of Mouth Marketing Association Web site, http://womma.org). The association goes on to say that word-of-mouth marketing "is the art and science of building active, mutually beneficial consumer-to-consumer and consumer-to-marketer communications."

Similar to the IMC principle that two-way communication is key to ensuring effective communication, WOMMA believes that all good word-of-mouth marketing is a dialogue, and specifically one that is beneficial to both parties.

There have been a number of definitions of "buzz" published since the 1990s; each one is slightly different, but each focuses on the exchange of information between people. Buzz is different from word-of-mouth marketing, however, according to Rosen (2000), in that buzz represents an aggregate. It is "the sum of all comments about a certain product that are exchanged among people at any given time" (p. 7). This distinction between word-of-mouth marketing and buzz is important because buzz connotes a hum of activity, whereas word of mouth may occur only infrequently.

Buzz and word-of-mouth marketing are the same, however, in that they are both difficult, if not impossible, to control. There are agencies that will help organizations build buzz, but at a certain point the media might become part of the equation. Organizations must be savvy enough to know when the buzz is positive and needs to be harnessed for the organization's gain, and when the buzz is negative and needs to be indirectly controlled through public relations strategies.

Viral Marketing

Viral marketing is a technique popularized in 2004 when Miami-based advertising agency Crispin Porter Bogusky developed an online video titled "Subservient Chicken." Once produced, the video was delivered by the agency via e-mail, and over time it was forwarded by an interested and amused public. Another classic example of viral marketing took place at

Hotmail, which gave away free e-mail accounts. At the bottom of every outgoing message from a Hotmail account is a message: "Get your private, free email at http://www.hotmail.com." As a result of the response, Hotmail grew exponentially. What these two examples have in common is the way the message is spread—via the Internet, like a virus.

Lewczak defines viral marketing as "the use of marketing techniques that seek to exploit pre-existing social networks to produce exponential increases in brand awareness through viral processes comparative to that of an epidemic" (Lewczak 2006). He further explains the popular types of viral marketing that exist, including so-called forward-to-a-friend messages and "incentivized viral" messages. Forward-to-a-friend messages require a line at the end of the e-mail or Web site that asks people to pass the message along to others in their network. Incentivized viral messages encourage recipients to provide a friend or family's e-mail address in return for a reward.

Although very often confused with buzz, word of mouth, and even guerrilla marketing, viral marketing is a specific technique that employs the Web and its inherent social networks to spread a message quickly and exponentially. One important thing to keep in mind is that the Web can work very quickly—both for and against an organization—so it is incumbent upon the organization to control the message as much as possible.

Direct Marketing

The Direct Marketing Association defines direct marketing as "an interactive system of marketing which uses one or more interactive media to effect a measurable response and/or transaction at any location" (Scovotti and Spiller n.d.). There are two important components to this definition—namely, that direct marketing makes use of "interactive media," and that it has a "measurable response."

Interactive media refers to both the response required of the recipient and the level of involvement of the recipient. For example, a direct-mail appeal (such as a catalog or a letter package) arrives in a postal mailbox, a telemarketing appeal is delivered via the telephone, and an e-mail appeal is delivered to a person's e-mail inbox. While the medium may differ, each of these appeals asks the consumer to respond immediately and directly in some way, whether by mail, by phone, or through a Web site.

It is this immediate response that helps to make direct marketing measurable. Most promotional messages have rather latent effects: consumers see or hear a message, and they might respond attitudinally or behaviorally, but organizations do not know if the response resulted from the advertising. With direct marketing, the organization can immediately trace results back to the individual recipient of the message and thus know the success or failure of the campaign.

Outdoor

Outdoor advertising also goes by the name of "out-of-home" because it encompasses everything consumers see outside their residences. The Outdoor Advertising Association of America (OAAA) defines outdoor advertising as "billboards; but it also means street furniture and transit advertising . . . as well as other alternative formats" (Outdoor Advertising Association of America Web site). This definition reflects the reality that it might be easier to define what outdoor *is not* rather than what it is. Any promotional message that consumers experience in their external environments is considered outdoor, or out-of-home. This includes everything commuters see in the subway car, or as they wait for the bus or subway.

While billboards are the most prevalent form of outdoor advertising, they are probably also the form of promotion that has come under the heaviest attack. In the 1960s, First Lady Ladybird Johnson fought for the "beautification" of America, which included banning billboards from the nation's highways. Although she was never successful in abolishing all of them, many local municipalities across the country, particularly resort areas, have outlawed billboards over concerns for the character of the town.

Recently, the billboard industry has begun to harness the power of technology. There are now digital billboards that can be updated and changed every few seconds, rather than every week or every month. Because technology allows updates to happen so quickly, billboard companies have used the boards for public service, specifically for Amber Alerts, the official mass media notification of a missing child, and for news of a bridge collapse in Minneapolis in 2007.

Guerrilla Marketing

Jay Conrad Levinson is considered the "father of guerrilla marketing." He coined the term in the 1980s to refer to a type of marketing aimed at "achieving conventional goals, such as profits and joy, with unconventional methods, such as investing energy instead of money" (www.gmarketing.com). With guerrilla marketing, the focus is on spending a minimal budget to achieve the greatest end result, and not necessarily following traditional models of marketing communications. For this reason, creative thinking is the only real requirement, and sometimes this creativity has caused ethical concerns.

One of the first examples of guerrilla marketing to gain widespread negative attention was "Fake Tourist," a tactic employed Sony Ericsson Mobile Communications Ltd. The company hired sixty actors to visit the Empire State Building in New York and the Space Needle in Seattle and act as if they were actual tourists who wanted their pictures taken by a passerby. The camera they gave to the unsuspecting passerby was the company's T68i, an early mobile camera phone (Vranica 2002). The part of this scenario that raised ethical concerns was the lack of awareness on the part of the consumers that they were part of a marketing event. Some would argue, however, that a lack of consumer awareness of participation was exactly the point: after the encounter with the actors, these consumers were very likely to tell their friends about this cool new camera phone they saw at the Empire State Building.

Social Media

Social media is a fairly new, widely used yet evolving term. As a result, there is no widely accepted definition. Generally speaking, however, social media refers to "the use of electronic and Internet tools for the purpose of sharing and discussing information and experiences with other human beings in more efficient ways" ("It's Time We Defined Social Media" 2008). This includes Web sites as varied as blogs, Facebook, MySpace, and LinkedIn, where people can connect with one another in both social and professional contexts, but also file-sharing sites such as Shutterfly, Flickr, and YouTube, where the public can post and share photos and videos.

Although social media sites have yet to be proven singularly effective for promoting a visual identity on a large scale, they are worth discussing because of the potential to both help and hurt an organization's visual identity promotion efforts. Social media sites enable the individual users to control the content they post, which means the sites provide a tremendous outlet for the positive or disgruntled views of consumers.

Summary

The promotion of a visual identity needs to be consistent across media in order for stakeholders and the public to build positive associations with the identity. One way of ensuring that the visual identity remains consistent is to develop an IMC plan, which ensures two-way communication with consumers. IMC employs a variety of media and tactics that carry the same visual identity message. Some of the major types of tactics available as part of an IMC strategy include: advertising, public relations, product packaging, building interiors and exteriors, vehicles, direct marketing, and social media, among many others delineated above.

Case Study: Kitchens-by-Design Develops an Integrated Marketing Plan

Kitchens-by-Design was founded in the Boston area in 1991 by Bill and Matt Johnson, brothers who grew up learning custom cabinet design from their father, a master craftsman who supported his family by working as a finish carpenter for several homebuilders.

Kitchens-by-Design had flourished in its fifteen years of business, mainly through recommendations from happy former clients. The Johnson brothers never thought about marketing their business because they had enough work to keep them busy, without the hassles of having so much work that they were forced to hire extra help.

During the building boom of the early 2000s, the Johnson brothers had little time to think about the future of their business. They were consistently busy, and assumed they would be forever, or at least for as long as they wanted to be. Once the economy got a little tighter and work began to slow down, however, the Johnsons began to think about ways to promote their business to attract more clients. For the first time in 15 years, Kitchens-by-Design considered marketing itself.

Over the course of several months, the Johnsons tried to think up creative ways to market Kitchens-by-Design. Since the brothers had not budgeted for marketing, they were also trying to think of ideas that would not be cost prohibitive. They knew television advertising was probably out of their reach, but were having trouble thinking of any alternatives.

One day, in the middle of client meeting, it hit Bill Johnson that the best way to market the business was through satisfied customers, but he was not at all sure how to reach all of them. After the client meeting ended, Bill shared his idea with Matt, and after a few minutes of discussion, they had an idea.

Using old customer records, Bill and Matt were able to develop a database of approximately 400 former clients. The database included basic information, including name and address, but also information relevant to the job for which they had been hired, including house architectural style, year the house was built, the job's budget, and a picture of the finished cabinets. Using this information, Kitchens-by-Design was able to imagine a pretty clear picture of its client base—and who might benefit from its services in the future.

Once the database was complete, Bill and Matt Johnson thought about what else they would need to successfully market Kitchens-by-Design. If they used the database to send out a postcard to former clients, they would need a design for the postcard, and a logo to identify the company. Both of these were no problem: Kitchens-by-Design had a simple logo that had been used on invoices and proposals in the past, and the design for the postcard would be a simple blueprint design with copy that asked former clients to recommend Kitchens-by-Design to people they knew who were considering renovating their kitchens.

After two weeks of simple design and printing, Bill and Matt Johnson mailed the postcard to their 400 former clients, then sat back and waited for a flood of new business. After a month with no response from the postcard, the Johnson brothers decided to pursue alternative promotional strategies. They began to install a small wood plate inside one cabinet door at each client's house. It would include the Kitchens-by-Design name and logo. That way, Kitchens-by-Design would always be top-of-mind with clients, who might then be inclined to recommend the company to friends considering a new kitchen.

Another promotional idea included having refrigerator magnets printed. The Johnsons thought refrigerator magnets with the Kitchens-by-Design name, logo, and contact information would be a good way to spur discussion about the company as friends were touring the clients' new kitchens.

Friends in the carpentry business suggested to the Johnsons that they should consider paying for a booth at a home design expo, which is similar to a trade show for people searching for home renovation contractors, supplies, and ideas.

Finally, because of their limited marketing budget, the Johnsons wondered if there was anything the company could do to generate some "free publicity" for Kitchens-by-Design.

Case Discussion Questions

1. Discuss the process by which Kitchens-by-Design developed its database. What advice would you offer to Bill and Matt Johnson if you were asked to assess the quality of the database?
2. How viable are the Johnsons' ideas for marketing Kitchens-by-Design? Again, imagine that you are a marketing consultant hired by the company. What advice would you offer?
3. Kitchens-by-Design is looking to capitalize on some free publicity. What could the company do to ensure some positive press coverage?

Bibliography

Aaker, D.A. 1991. *Managing Brand Equity: Capitalizing on the Value of a Brand Name.* New York: Free Press.

Aaker, D.A., and E. Joachimsthaler, 2000. *Brand Leadership.* New York: Free Press.

Balasubramanian, S.K. 1994. "Beyond Advertising and Publicity: Hybrid Messages and Public Policy Issues." *Journal of Advertising* 23 (Fall): 29–46.

Balasubramanian, S.K., J.A. Karrh, and H. Patwardhan. 2006. "Audience Response to Product Placements: An Integrative Framework and Future Research Agenda." *Journal of Advertising* 35, no. 3: 115–141.

Burnett, J., and S. Moriarty. 1998. *Introduction to Marketing Communications: An Integrated Approach.* Upper Saddle River, NJ: Prentice-Hall.

Cornelissen, J.P., and A.R. Lock. 2000. "Theoretical Concept or Management Fashion? Examining the Significance of IMC." *Journal of Advertising Research* 40, no. 5: 7–15.

Cutlip, S., A. Center, and G. Broom. 1994. *Effective Public Relations.* Englewood Cliffs:, NJ Prentice-Hall.

Fannin, R. 1983. "Diary of an Amazing Comeback." *Marketing and Media Decisions* 18 (Spring): 129–134.

Goodyear Blimp Web site. www.goodyearblimp.com.

Gray, J.G., Jr. 1986. *Managing the Corporate Image: The Key to Public Trust.* Westport, CT: Quorum Books.

Guerrilla Marketing Association Web site. www.gmarketing.com.

"It's Time We Defined Social Media. No More Arguing. Here's the Definition." 2008. Benparr.com: Internet Tools and Innovation. Available at www.benparr.com/2008/08/its-time-we-defined-social-media-no-more-arguing-heres-the-definition. Accessed December 12, 2008.

Keller, K.L. 1996. "Brand Equity and Integrated Communication." In *Integrated*

Communication: Synergy of Persuasive Voices, ed. E. Thorson and J. Moore. Mahwah, NJ: Lawrence Erlbaum Associates.

————. 1998. *Strategic Brand Management: Building, Measuring, and Managing Brand Equity.* Upper Saddle River, NJ: Prentice-Hall.

Lambert, A. 1989. "Corporate Identity and Facilities Management." *Facilities* 7, no. 12: 7–12.

Lewczak, J.J. 2006. "Viral, 'Buzz' and 'Stealth' Marketing." American Marketing Association. Available at www.marketingpower.com/content33908.php. Accessed April 28, 2009.

Markwick, N., and C. Fill. 1997. "Towards a Framework for Managing Corporate Identity." *European Journal of Marketing* 31, nos. 5–6: 396–409.

Melewar, T.C. 2001. "Measuring Visual Identity: A Multi-Construct Study." *Corporate Communications: An International Journal* 5, no. 1: 36–41.

Meyers, H.M., and M.J. Lubliner. 1998. *The Marketer's Guide to Successful Package Design.* Chicago: NTC Business Books.

Olson, E.M., R. Cooper, and S.F. Slater. 1998. "Design Strategy and Competitive Advantage." *Business Horizons* 41, no. 2: 55–61.

Outdoor Advertising Association of America Web site. www.oaaa.org.

Pratt, M.G., and A. Rafaeli. 1997. "Organizational Dress as a Symbol of Multilayered Social Identities." *Academy of Management Journal* 40, no. 4: 862–898.

Richards, J.I., and C.M. Curran. 2002. "Oracles on "Advertising": Searching for a Definition." *Journal of Advertising* 31, no. 2: 63–77.

Rosen, E. 2000. *The Anatomy of Buzz: How to Create Word of Mouth Marketing.* New York: Doubleday.

Schmitt, B., and A. Simonson. 1997. *Marketing Aesthetics: The Strategic Management of Brands, Identity, and Image.* New York: Free Press.

Schultz, D., G. Kerr, H. Kim, and C. Patti. 2007. "In Search of a Theory of Integrated Marketing Communication." *Journal of Advertising Education* 11, no. 2: 21–31.

Schultz, D.E., and P.J. Kitchen. 2000. "A Response to 'Theoretical Concept or Management Fashion?'" *Journal of Advertising Research* 40, no. 5: 17–21.

Schultz, D.E., S.I. Tannenbaum, and R.F. Lauterborn. 1993. *Integrated Marketing Communications: Pulling It Together and Making It Work.* Chicago: NTC Business Books.

Scovotti, C. and L.D. Spiller. n.d. "Revisiting the Conceptual Definition of Direct Marketing: Perspectives from Scholars and Practitioners." Working Paper. Available at www.the-dma.org/index.php. Accessed January 23, 2008.

Siomkos, G.J. 1992. "Conceptual and Methodological Propositions for Assessing Responses to Industrial Crises." *Review of Business* 13, no. 4: 26–31.

Vranica, S. 2002. "That Guy Showing Off His Hot New Phone May Be a Shill— New Campaign for Sony Ericsson Puts Actors in Real-Life Settings; Women Play Battleship at the Bar." *Wall Street Journal*, July 31, p. B1.

White, J. 1992. *Two Pesos, Inc. v. Taco Cabana, Inc.* 505 U.S. 763. 1992 LEXIS 4533.

Word of Mouth Marketing Association Web site. www.womma.org.

3

Developing and Launching a New Visual Identity

Developing a new visual identity is a task undertaken with the development of a new organization, a change in an organization's name due to a merger or acquisition, or even the start of events, such as the Olympic Games. The Olympic Games will be held in London in 2012, and the planning of the event began almost as soon as the city was awarded the games in 2005.

Part of the planning for the games includes designing a host city–specific logo for use in promotion both before and during the games. The logo for London 2012 was unveiled in mid-2007, so the plan was to use it for five years even before the games began, as a way of building some equity around the logo and the games themselves. Once the games begin, the logo designed by the host city is typically pervasive: it appears in the media, on the venues, and on all of the apparel and novelty items sold in association with the games. The logo is meant to instill pride in the host city and provide a rallying point for the rest of the world. This was not the reaction, however, when the London 2012 logo was unveiled in the summer of 2007.

London 2012

The London 2012 logo was designed by London-based identity consultancy Wolff Olins at a cost of approximately $800,000 (Sullivan 2007). Developers unveiled the logo with the understanding that one goal of the London organizing committee was to appeal to young people and get them excited about the Olympic Games. The logo was described as:

> A chunky, graffiti-style depiction of the number "20" stacked above the number "12," looking a bit like a jagged piece of popcorn, incorporating

the Olympic rings and the word "London" in lowercase letters . . . in vivid blue, green, orange and pink versions, each with a bright yellow outline, which organizers said was meant to appeal especially to young people. (Sullivan 2007).

The design included the logo itself as well as an "identity system," a set of directions on using the logo in various media and various colors. This is an important element of any visual identity development because the elements will be used in a number of sizes, in a number of colors, and in a number of media, both those prevalent when the logo was designed and also any emerging media. In addition, a video aired on national television to accompany the unveiling of the logo. It featured "an animated image of a diver whose entry into the water sent out ripples of sparkling, flashing lights" (Murphy 2007). A broadcast or video presentation of a logo is not unusual, but in the case of London 2012, the video triggered epileptic seizures in at least twenty-three people with photosensitive epilepsy (Murphy 2007).

When the new logo itself was unveiled, it was accompanied by public outcry from a core group of detractors, which is fairly typical, since most high-profile organizations expect a certain amount of public outcry and private disdain with the unveiling of a new identity. What the London 2012 committee likely did not expect was the passionate reaction, almost all of it negative.

The cadre of people who reacted negatively to the logo included public officials, columnists, and the general public. Approximately 50,000 people signed an online petition to do away with the logo, saying it looked like "bad graffiti" or even a "broken swastika." Several members of Parliament also signed a motion in an attempt to force the committee to abandon the design (Leong 2007).

London mayor Ken Livingstone, who had originally defended the logo, reacted strongly when the video version caused a health concern. The mayor stated: "I wouldn't pay them a penny. Who would go to a firm like that again to ask them to do that work? If you employ someone to design a logo for you and they haven't done a basic health check, you have to ask what they do for their money" (Leong 2007). A London Assembly member and the Conservative spokesperson for the 2012 Games described the logo as "hideous." "Questions need to be answered as to how we have ended up in this situation. Was there an open competition to supply the designs? If so, what on earth do the rejected ones look like?"

(Leong 2007). Even the founder of London's Design Museum told the press that the logo "is a puerile mess, an artistic flog and a commercial scandal. . . . It is feeble. It was a wonderful chance to do something magnificent, and it was a waste of resources" (Sullivan 2007).

The founder of London's Design Museum aside, generally, those who know design and understand the nuances of creating a visual identity— and those involved in the development of the identity—defended the logo. Michael Wolff of Wolff Olins, the agency that designed the logo, defended the choice by lashing out at detractors: "Prejudice is comfortable and lazy. I think most of us will come to see this symbol as a breakthrough" (Leong 2007).

Sebastian Coe, a former British distance runner who headed the organizing committee, was quoted widely in the press defending the logo:

> We don't do bland. This is not a bland city, and we were not going to come out with a bland corporate logo that would just be left to appear on a polo shirt you do your gardening in in a few weeks. . . . We believe we have got something that will live, something that will help us as we approach the Games, something with an international feel and something that will help us with business. (Sullivan 2007)

A dean at the University of Toronto's Joseph L. Rotman School of Management told the press that identity consultancy Wolff Olins "did their homework. . . . There is some science to it. They're going after a specific target market and the ones who are complaining are probably not in this target market" (Leong 2007).

The Cost of a New Visual Identity

Any visual identity—whether a new organization is developing its first or is relaunching a new one—comes with certain fixed costs. Generally speaking, these fixed costs can be broken down into five categories: consultant fees, cost of creating new materials, cost of the launch, replacement costs (for a visual identity relaunch), and the cost for developing new systems within the organization, such as those associated with human resources or purchasing (Olins and Selame 1993).

The cost of a visual identity launch for a given organization will depend on a number of variables, including the organization's budget, but each visual identity launch has several things in common, including the

necessity of exploring what visual identity will best suit the organization's mission and strategy. This is best accomplished through rigorous
research.

Secondary Research

Secondary research can be helpful to organizations with budget constraints because they may be able to apply the lessons learned by other
organizations to their own. Secondary research can also teach an organization a great deal about color and typography, two important components of any visual identity, since both can be used to influence people's
associations with an organization's visual identity.

Color Theory

Holtzschue (2006) writes: "Color is stimulating, calming, expressive,
disturbing, impressional [*sic*], cultural, exuberant, symbolic. It pervades
every aspect of our lives . . . good color can determine [a product's]
success or failure in the consumer market . . . color means business"
(p. 2).

Holtzschue refers to color theory as being two-pronged. It is the con-
vergence of the quest for a color-order system and the search for harmony
in color combinations. On a practical level, the study of color focuses on
three areas: learning to distinguish the many qualities of different colors,
learning to understand the "instability" of color—given that colors appear
differently depending on the light, where they are placed relative to other
colors, and in which medium they are placed—and learning to develop
consistently effective color combinations (Holtzschue 2006).

The Business of Color

The "business of color," otherwise known as commercial color-order
systems, provides efficiency and consistency to the design process, which
benefits organizations developing visual identities. The Pantone Matching
System (PMS) is one of the most widely used commercial color-order
systems. It provides "a palette of standardized colors for a wide range
of products, ranging from printer inks to software, color films, plastics,
and markers" (Holtzschue 2006, p. 8). Each of the colors has a unique
identification number that corresponds to a formula for mixing the proper

inks to make that color; graphic designers use the PMS swatch books during the design phase to ensure color consistency.

Most organizations have a specific color that is used on every piece of communication. This ensures consistency across media and over time, but it also simplifies the process of working with outside designers and vendors because PMS numbers eliminate any confusion between the organization and the vendor or designer regarding a color's hue or shade.

When Tiffany and Co. orders a new print run of its famous "Tiffany Blue" boxes, the ink used to print them is known as PMS 1837. Regardless which printing company actual prints the boxes, the use of PMS 1837 will ensure that the ink color is consistent and matches all of the boxes printed previously. In this way, the PMS color system ensures the integrity of an organization's color palette. (Coincidentally, 1837 is also the year Tiffany and Co. was founded.)

Typography

Just as color can set a tone and affect a person's associations with a visual identity, typography—or fonts—can have a profound effect on what a person thinks of a visual identity. Peterson (1996) writes: "When a letterform is flowing and curvaceous, the feeling conveyed is softer than the feeling communicated when the letterform is angular and hard-edged. A whimsical letterform will convey a light-hearted mood; one that is elegant will communicate sophistication" (p. 31).

To illustrate how two typefaces can have a very different effect, look at Table 3.1 and determine which of the typefaces is more appropriate given the meaning of the words.

Typefaces typically fit into one of four categories: serif, sans serif, display, and script.

Table 3.1

Typeface Associations

FAT	fat
SKINNY	skinny

Serif. Serif typefaces have been around since ancient times. They contain short lines, often called hooks, stemming from the ends of the letters. Serif typefaces are often used as body copy, or for long blocks of text, such as in newspapers. The body copy used in this book is an example of a serif font, and these font types are often the most legible typefaces (Peterson 1996).

Sans Serif. Sans serif typefaces are so named because they do *not* contain the serifs of serif typefaces. "Sans" is from the French for "without." This kind of typeface is very simple and straightforward, so sans serif typefaces are typically used for headlines and captions (Peterson 1996).

Display. Display typefaces are generally used for decoration rather than legibility. Because they tend to be ornate, a display typeface is never used in body copy (Peterson 1996). Most logotypes would be considered display typefaces.

Script. Script typefaces resemble calligraphy or very fancy handwriting. Because they are ornate and often difficult to read, script typefaces are never used as body copy. They are often used on ceremonial communications, such as wedding invitations.

Primary Research

While the wealth of secondary research available can provide an organization with a lot of useful information related to developing a visual identity, a more effective approach to visual identity research is to conduct primary research that is specifically focused on the organization and tailored to its objectives. If the organization has elected to hire an outside consultant or agency to develop its visual identity, the consultant will conduct primary research. If the organization is undertaking its visual identity launch without the help of an outside consultant, it will need to ensure that it conducts the appropriate type of research to suit its strategic vision for the visual identity.

There are many types of primary research methods available, but below is a discussion of several of the most widely used in marketing: focus groups, ethnography, and survey.

Focus Groups

A focus group is, according to Krueger and Casey (2000), "a special type of group in terms of purpose, size, composition, and procedures. The purpose of [forming] a focus group is to listen and gather information. It is a way to better understand how people feel or think about an issue, product, or service" (p. 5).

Krueger and Casey (2000) outline the criteria that define a focus group: the people chosen for the group must be in a focused discussion led by a moderator; each person must possess a common characteristic that is relevant to the objective of the focus group; and finally, the group must yield qualitative data that helps the researchers understand the topic being studied.

Traditionally, focus groups have been the research method of choice for agencies and consultants working in the consumer realm. More recently, however, the focus group has fallen out of favor, with some arguing that focus groups do not accurately reflect consumer thinking.

The argument that focus groups have become less likely to provide useful consumer data stems from the feeling that the groups are contrived: focus group conversations are not representative of actual consumer conversations. Also, consumers have become savvy enough to know that focus groups are designed to collect data, so consumer responses might be tailored to fit what they think the researchers want to hear.

There are many who still believe in the efficacy of focus groups, particularly in the case of exploring design and naming ideas. The problem arises when focus groups are used to validate or invalidate existing research.

Ethnography

Ethnography began as an anthropological research method. It calls for researchers to immerse themselves in a culture other than their own in order to intensively observe—and perhaps participate in—the culture, and to "make the psychological transference whereby 'they' becomes 'we'" (Elliott and Jankel-Elliott 2003, p. 216). By changing the context from "they" to "we," researchers are best able to understand the way others live their lives. Over time, consumer researchers adopted and adapted the ethnographic approach to study consumer culture rather than indigenous cultures.

In a consumer-focused ethnography, researchers observe the "culture" of product brands or categories. This is the major philosophical difference between the anthropological approach and the marketing approach, but there are also logistical differences. In a consumer-focused marketing ethnography, researchers might observe consumer groups for shorter amounts of time and videotape the interactions. In some cases, these taped "field notes" can become a part of the organization's campaign. One example is the "Having a baby changes everything" campaign by Johnson & Johnson. The black-and-white advertisements aired on television were actually part of the video footage shot by the research team.

Survey

A survey, or questionnaire, is a research tool whose components include a carefully constructed set of questions aimed at eliciting information from consumers (Davis 1996). Surveys are administered on a wide scale to a random sample of participants that fit the organization's target audience, and the results can be analyzed quantitatively and generalized to the larger population.

Surveys can be helpful in a number of situations and contexts, but they can be especially helpful when an organization's researchers are seeking to validate or invalidate previous qualitative research. Finding out whether the results of previous research are valid can save the organization both time and money in the development of a new visual identity.

Visual Identity Launches

Nike

Research can play a very important role in the development of any or all elements of a visual identity, but not all organizations come about their names in such a systematic way. One of today's most famous brand names, formerly "Dimension Six" and "Blue Ribbon Sports," became Nike as the result of a dream and was launched in a fairly uneventful way.

Jeff Johnson, Nike's first official employee, had a dream about Nike, the goddess of victory who presided over Greece alongside Zeus. Nike founder Phil Knight agreed to the name, commissioned a logo—the

"Swoosh"—from a graphic design student for $35, and the new brand debuted in 1972 at Olympic trials in Eugene, Oregon (Krentzman 1997).

LG Electronics Launches in the United States

Korea-based LG Electronics was launched in 1958 to sell consumer electronics and home appliances, and has since expanded into mobile communications. In 1999, LG bought U.S.-based Zenith Corporation, and in 2003 LG launched itself in the United States with the intention of becoming one of the top three consumer electronics companies in the world by 2010.

The slogan of LG, "Life's Good," reinforces the corporate name by employing the "LG" in both the name and the logo. According to the company's Web site, "Life's Good" is meant to convey to consumers that using LG brands will add to their quality of life. To reinforce the notion of quality of life in its own visual identity, the company adopted a logo that personifies happiness:

> The stylized image of the human face consists of the letters L and G, the circular nature of the image represents the world, future, youth, humanity, and technology, and the red stands for friendliness and commitment. (LG Web site, www.lge.com)

Ogilvy PR managed LG's U.S. launch, the centerpiece of which was "Pucker Up New York," which attracted 100 media professionals from major outlets, such as the *New York Times*, *Forbes*, *Maxim*, *Popular Science*, *Us Weekly*, the "Today Show," and MTV. The campaign focused on a branded LG digital billboard in Times Square that featured images of New Yorkers kissing. The campaigned was previewed on CBS's "The Early Show," thousands of people interacted with the billboard, and more than 100 stories about the campaign appeared in the print, broadcast, and online press. Ogilvy PR estimated the advertising equivalency at $3.2 million (Ogilvy PR Case Studies n.d.).

Google: From Simple Logotype to "Dynamic Identity"

Shortly after Larry Page and Sergey Brin launched their Google search engine in 1998, the two men left Silicon Valley for the Burning Man

Festival in Nevada. To let Google users know where they were, Page and Brin drew representative images of the festival into the brightly colored Google logotype (Rawsthorn 2007). With their actions, the Google Doodle was launched. Every major holiday, Google users see a slight variation of the Google logotype celebrating the specific holiday. Rawsthorn refers to this type of logo as a "dynamic identity," and defines dynamic identities as "symbols that adopt different guises at different times or in different contexts, so you're never sure exactly how they'll look" (p. 10). While a visual identity that changes defies the idea that consistency is key in promoting a visual identity, one could argue that the very fact of Google having a dynamic identity—one that actually maintains the basic integrity of the core logotype—actually reinforces the Google identity.

United Negro College Fund Becomes UNCF

In early 2008, the United Negro College Fund, a minority education assistance organization, officially changed its name to UNCF. At the same time, it adopted a more stylized torch logo and updated its color palette. Its tagline, "A mind is a terrible thing to waste" remained unchanged.

UNCF worked for four years to develop its new visual identity, part-nering with notable consultants Young and Rubicam, McKinsey and Co., and Landor Associates. The chief marketing officer at UNCF remarked on the change:

> Revitalizing the UNCF brand was an inspiring challenge. . . . It is one of the most iconic brands in America, with an incredibly rich history and a strong record of success. We worked hard to ensure the new identity was respectful of UNCF's pioneering heritage, while, at the same time, celebrating its expanding role as the leading voice for minority education. ("United Negro College Fund Revitalizes Its Brand" 2008).

The official launch of the new visual identity took place at Spelman College, one of the UNCF's most prominent member colleges. To gen-erate more national awareness of the visual identity change, the UNCF sponsored its annual "Evening of Stars" with Smokey Robinson on BET, and television and print public service announcements carrying the new visual identity were developed by Young and Rubicam and co-branded with the Ad Council.

Court TV Becomes truTV

During December 2007, cable television viewers began to see ads announcing the launch of *truTV*, a rebranding of the former *CourtTV*. The launch was set for January 1, 2008, so December was devoted to alerting viewers to the change. The new network, using the tagline "Not Reality. Actuality," promised viewers real people in real situations "from an exciting and dramatic first-person perspective" (*truTV* Web site, www.trutv.com). This represented a dramatic change in format, but the network's change in its visual identity was only minor. The typeface for *CourtTV* remained, and the network simply reversed the last three letters of "court" to become "tru." This minor change in identity has the potential to signal to viewers that they can expect only minor changes in the network's programming.

jetBlue

The team developing the start-up airline now known as jetBlue had been struggling to find just the right name. Founder and CEO David Neeleman wanted the word "blue" either as the airline's name or in the airline's name. Trademarking such a generic term, however, would have proven difficult. In discussing the name with Neeleman, the new airline's corporate communications manager kept suggesting ways of incorporating "blue" into the name. "'I just kept babbling,' she said, 'and I said, you can call it 'fly blue' or you could call it 'jet blue' or you could . . . 'Jet Blue' conjured seemingly from nowhere, was, clearly, what they'd been groping for." Later that evening, the communications manager sketched out a simple logotype on a napkin and the brand was born (Peterson 2004).

Style Guides

Concurrently with the development and launch of a visual identity, many organizations will begin to think seriously about the conditions under which the organization's visual identity elements can and should be used. This is an important step in the visual identity development process for two reasons: rules regarding the use of visual identity elements help to build consistency in the use of the identity, and consistency in the use of the identity helps to protect the visual identity from misuse and infringement.

The set rules dictating the use of an organization's visual identity elements are typically codified in what is referred to as a visual identity manual or corporate style guide (Allen 1995). These manuals are dense compilations of rules pertaining to the proper use of an organization's name, logo, tagline, color palette (including the use of specific PMS colors), and other elements of its visual identity. Many organizations develop guides as a way of ensuring the proper use of their visual identities by employees, vendors, the media, and the public:

> Good design saves time and money and enhances communication and understanding. And that is what a graphics standards manual helps to do. It is based on considerable research, analysis, surveying, interviewing, and validating—to tailor a visual communication system to an agency's unique needs. (Blackburn 1976)

Some firms choose to place visual identity standards online, since the Web provides a more user-friendly way to present corporate identity standards. In addition, online standards are easier to update and provide worldwide access, which may go a long way toward ensuring consistency among the employees and agencies (Frook 2000).

In larger organizations, there might also be someone whose job includes enforcing the "logo rules," as they are sometimes called. Lorge (1998) interviewed one self-proclaimed "chief of logo police" who lamented the tedious work frequently associated with educating employees on the importance of presenting a consistent visual identity:

> I try desperately to have people understand they should follow the identity rules. If you don't, you're compromising the brand image. . . . It's a continuing task to get folks to understand why it's important. I simply explain that every time you see the Lear logo, it's an exposure. It works singly, but it also works cumulatively. Don't compromise it; [if you do] you're destroying the synergy of the program. (p. 42)

The External Launch of a New Visual Identity

The strategy behind launching a new visual identity will differ depending on many organizational factors, including the size and scope of the organization, whether the organization is nonprofit or for profit, whether the organization is local or global, and whether it is public or private. These factors will dictate changes in the budget and scope of the launch, but many other tactics will remain constant from organization to organization, and organizations of all sizes need to consider both external and internal launch issues.

Media Announcements

Organizations of all sizes and scopes should consider announcing the launch of a new visual identity to the media. The media can include both the mainstream and trade press. If either the mainstream or trade press picks up the news of the visual identity launch, the organization is able to achieve a level of news saturation using public relations without incurring the large cost of launching the visual identity through the media's advertising channels. Of course, the newsworthiness of a visual identity launch is going to be judged by the media itself: smaller organizations without a broad reach may be at a disadvantage, whereas the launch of a new visual identity by large corporation might be deemed highly newsworthy.

Research by Lippincott and Margulies (White 2000) found that firms using the media to announce a new company name at the time of a merger announcement actually benefited from advertising value equivalency (AVE). Jeffries-Fox (2003) defines AVE this way:

> AVEs are calculated by measuring the column inches (in the case of print), or seconds (in the case of broadcast media), and multiplying these figures by the respective medium's advertising rates (per inch or per second). The resulting number is what it would have cost to place an advertisement of that size in that medium. By assessing all of your media coverage in this way, and aggregating all such calculations, you can assign an overall AVE to your coverage within a certain time period.

The value of this study is clear: announcing the name change at the time of the merger, rather than days, weeks, or months afterward, allows firms to take advantage of the media's desire to cover the merger, while potentially cutting the cost to formally advertise the name change later (White 2000).

While free press coverage of a name change is of tremendous value to any organization, many scholars question the validity of advertising equivalency measures. They contend that the opportunity to buy advertising in space that has been specifically allocated to editorial coverage does not exist. The Lippincott and Margulies study strongly suggests, however, that newly merged firms may be missing out on opportunities to communicate their new names to the public simply as a result of poor timing.

Advertising the New Visual Identity

Gaining valuable media attention at no direct charge to the organization is an enviable element of any organizational visual identity launch, but the organization must be large or important enough in the eyes of the media to garner such attention. Because not every organization will be able to count on this publicity as part of its launch, many organizations might find it necessary to pay to advertise their new visual identities.

When deciding on an advertising strategy for launching the new visual identity, there are a number of factors to consider: message, audience, media, and timing. Each is discussed in more detail below.

Message

The message concerning a new visual identity might seem obvious, but the audience seeing the advertising of a new identity might have more questions than you've considered. For example, rather than just knowing *what* the new identity is or means, the audience will want to know *why* the visual identity has been developed—or changed, if that is the case.

Audience

The external audience for your message is an important consideration. Employees will be addressed in the internal launch, but they will undoubtedly see any advertising directed toward the external audience, so the messages in both launches should be consistent. The major audience for the external launch, however, will probably encompass several different groups depending on the type of organization, including customers, investors, donors, vendors, and regulators. Each of these audiences might require a slightly different message consistent with their affiliation with the organization.

Media

The audience for the organization's visual identity message should dictate the medium or media used to reach them. The considerations for media choice will undoubtedly include budget and timing, but thought should also be given to the best way to reach these audiences. Mainstream newspapers and broadcast television provide broad reach, but the costs might be prohibitive. More targeted publications and trade publications can provide a niche audience at a more reasonable price point.

Timing

The question of *when* to announce the launch of a new visual identity should be addressed as part of the overall launch strategy. For example, should the external launch happen simultaneously with the internal launch? If not, how far in advance should the internal launch precede the external launch? In some cases, the deadlines associated with various media might dictate the timing of the advertising associated with the launch, but it is best to develop an overall launch strategy and then rework it as needed depending on media deadlines.

The Internal Launch of a New Visual Identity

If an organization is adopting a new visual identity, an internal launch is a natural—and necessary—step in unveiling the new program. The internal launch can also help to build momentum for the external launch if employees are motivated to spread the word about the new visual identity.

An internal launch is a logistical challenge because it involves both publicity and event planning. If the organization is international or global in nature, the internal launch will also involve trying to coordinate the official launch timing. Regardless of how the official launch is timed, there are a number of very basic elements that should be a part of any internal visual identity launch.

CEO-led Employee Meeting

An organization's visual identity should be managed at the organization's most senior level, so news of a launch should come from those managing the visual identity. If possible, the most senior person in the organization (preferably the CEO or equivalent person) should convene a meeting of all employees. The reason for involvement at such a high level is that employee perceptions matter. Because visual identity is a strategic issue, it is imperative that employees see it as something important enough to be addressed by the CEO.

If the organization is global, or even just has a number of offices in different locations, employees who are unable to attend the meeting should be able to view it via teleconference or streaming video online. Regardless of how employees view it, this meeting should be devoted entirely to discussing the new visual identity—why it was developed, its meaning, and why it is important to the organization.

To promote the meeting itself, the organization should use a variety of employee communications channels—the organization's intranet, employee newsletters, fliers, in-house closed-circuit television, and so on—to make contact with employees through several media.

If the organization publishes an official newsletter, whether print or online, a prominent story on the new visual identity would serve two purposes: it would alert employees to the identity-launch meeting, and it could go into greater detail about the meaning of the identity, which would educate employees on its importance.

Brand Book

At the CEO-led meeting, it is beneficial for employees to receive a "takeaway," an informational piece that employees can refer to later for information on the visual identity. This takeaway—also called a "brand book"—can also serve to educate future employees.

The actual format and production quality of the brand book can vary depending on the organization's budget, but at a minimum it should contain a mission statement, an organizational history, a discussion of why specific elements of the visual identity (name, logo, and colors) were chosen, and any other interesting facts that seem appropriate. The book should also describe, in as much detail as possible, the meaning behind the identity. If time is short and printing the booklet is not an option, post it on the organization's intranet and project the page and URL on a screen during the employee meeting.

Visual Metaphor

The brand book helps to bring an abstract idea (the meaning of the visual identity) to life through the use of visual metaphors (the actual visual identity). An even more effective way to do this is through the use of moving images on DVD or video. If time and budget permit, showing this DVD at the employee meeting can help to bring the visual identity alive.

The DVD is also a way to energize the organization as it embarks on its visual identity launch. It should be a montage of photos (of employees in the workplace, from movies, TV, or even magazines) set to music that captures the meaning of the identity and the culture it represents. This is a way to give the visual identity a personality, but it is also effective as a visual point of reference. That said, it is very important to carefully choose only those visuals that are truly representative of the organization's attributes, as employees may begin to "model" the visual identity based on an image they saw on the DVD. This DVD is also a good tool for future employee orientation sessions. When presented in combination with the brand book produced for the all-employee meeting, the DVD can give new employees an energetic introduction to the organization's visual identity, history, and culture.

Specialty Advertising (Giveaways)

Finally, as a thank-you to employees for coming to the meeting, and as a way of letting them know they are an integral part of the future of the visual identity, consider ordering t-shirts in the organization's color that are embroidered or silk-screened with the name, logo, and tagline. Each time an employee wears the t-shirt out in public, your organization is guaranteed wide exposure. Another way to provide a more consistent level of internal exposure to the visual identity is through specialty items such as pens, mugs, and mouse pads.

Summary

Organizations should conduct some form of research before embarking on the development and launch of a new visual identity. Research on color theory and typography can teach organizations a great deal about existing associations with colors and typefaces. Generally, secondary research can also help organizations apply the lessons learned by other organizations. If the budget permits, a focused primary research program can be helpful in tailoring a program that fits the organization's visual identity needs. Some of the most widely used forms of primary research in marketing include focus groups, ethnography, and survey.

Once the visual identity has been developed, the organization needs to develop a set of guidelines outlining how and when the organization's visual identity elements can be used. These guidelines are codified in a "style guide," and this guide helps to build consistency in the use of the identity. In turn, consistency in the use of the identity helps to protect the visual identity from misuse and infringement.

When launching the identity, plans need to be made to launch both externally and internally. The external launch of a new visual identity should include the basic elements of a media announcement and advertisements announcing the new visual identity. Advertisements will need to consider the message, the audience, the appropriate media vehicles, and the timing of the message.

The internal launch of a new visual identity means ensuring that employees are educated about the identity itself, but also the reasons the organization is launching a new visual identity. As when launching externally, there are basic tactics that should be a part of any internal launch: a meeting for employees led by the CEO, or the most senior person in the organization; a brand book that educates employees on the meaning of the visual identity; and some type of specialty advertising or promotional piece that employees can take with them, such as a t-shirt, mug, or mouse pad, to serve as a constant reminder of the new visual identity.

Case Study: The Spasiba Foundation Launches Nationally

The Spasiba Foundation was founded by wealthy philanthropist Jennifer Jackson, the adoptive mother of several Russian orphans, to provide funding and other resources to orphanages in Moscow. Just six months after its founding, Jackson made arrangements to acquire a small U.S.-based adoption agency. The agency had an established relationship with several Moscow orphanages and had placed thousands of children with families in the United States.

Jackson's vision for the Spasiba Foundation included serving as a type of full-service philanthropy, one that could help the children in Moscow while also bringing at least some of them together with American parents. Jackson saw this acquisition as a way to truly improve the lives of Russian orphans both in the United States and in Moscow.

Jackson was widely praised in the press and respected by foundation employees for her focus on improving the lives of children who would otherwise go unnoticed, but her business acumen was criticized privately: employees felt as if acquiring the adoption agency was too much too soon for the small foundation.

Because she wanted to provide as much assistance as possible to the Russian orphans, part of Jackson's dream included launching the Spasiba Foundation nationally in the United States, which she announced to the press in March along with the announcement of the adoption agency acquisition.

Over the next several months, integration of the two organizations proved difficult, given the specific nuances of both and the legal and international red tape associated with doing business across borders. The most difficult part of the integration from a marketing perspective was the question of visual identity.

Before the acquisition of the adoption agency, the Spasiba Foundation and the adoption agency each had distinctive logos, but they were very different from each other, given each organization's purpose. The legacy Spasiba Foundation logo consisted of both type and a rectangular graphic element: "Spasiba Foundation" was written in a Cyrillic-style typeface in an arch against the blue, white, and red stripes on the Russian flag. The adoption agency's logo was rather complex: it was a circle with an adult hand holding a child's hand, which was superimposed over a map, with the child's hand extending from Russia and the adult's hand extending from the United States. The name of the adoption agency was written in a serif typeface below the circle.

The marketing manager for the Spasiba Foundation and the founder of the adoption agency, who would become a public affairs manager in the Spasiba Foundation, met in May, two months after the announcement of the acquisition, to discuss the launch issues. The new organization would continue to be known as the Spasiba Foundation, but questions remained concerning how the logo would reflect the foundation's new efforts with regard to international adoption. Most of the discussion focused on which legacy logo to adopt—that of the Spasiba Foundation or the adoption agency—for the Spasiba Foundation, or whether an entirely new logo was necessary, but there was no resolution to the issue as spring became summer.

By July, the marketing team was struggling with the tactical communication problems associated with having no definitive visual identity. They were directed to always use Helvetica as the foundation's typeface, since it was simple, but there was no other visual guide. To avoid confusion, and because employees had emotional connections to their "legacy" identities, the Spasiba Foundation's employees used the logo they had always used, and the adoption agency employees continued to use their agency's old logo alongside the Spasiba Foundation name. As a result, there was tremendous inconsistency in the materials that went out to donors and prospective parents.

The delay in launching a new, official logo was due both to logistical and cultural differences. The Spasiba Foundation's top marketing manager had been tasked with finding a design agency to develop the foundation's new logo and typeface treatments. After receiving the logos and narrowing the choices down to three, however, all employees were asked to vote for their favorite: employees who had always worked for the Spasiba Foundation chose one logo and those employees who came from the adoption agency chose another. Eventually, the marketing manager asked Jennifer Jackson to choose the new logo. She chose the third option.

With three logos and no clear "winner," Jackson made the executive decision to employ the logo she liked best: one that looked remarkably similar to the legacy logo of the Spasiba Foundation. With a definitive logo chosen, Jackson asked the marketing manager and public affairs manager to develop a set of guidelines for using the logo.

It was December, nine months after Jackson had announced the acquisition of the adoption agency and the national launch of the Spasiba Foundation, before marketing employees received a copy of the visual identity style guide, which outlined how the visual identity could and should be employed in various media. The guidelines had been developed and issued rather hastily to employees via the foundation's intranet, since Jackson wanted to finalize the marketing issues that had lingered since March.

From a practical perspective, having the guidelines online allowed the foundation to refine them as time went on. The guidelines were also intentionally flexible so that employees could adapt them for use in a variety of emerging media, but this built-in flexibility also threatened to leave the guidelines open to interpretation. Employees were pleased that the foundation now had an official visual identity, but they were surprised to see a logo that was nearly identical to the Spasiba Foundation's legacy logo.

The national launch of the Spasiba Foundation was set for April 15, nearly thirteen months after Jackson had announced the acquisition and her intention to launch the foundation nationally. The foundation planned an internal launch to build excitement and momentum for the national launch.

The national launch plan included a large press conference, with Jackson lauding the work of the foundation and the new adoption services it would provide to help link Russian orphans with prospective American parents. She invited foundation donors as well as parents who had adopted their children through the adoption agency. In addition, Jackson did one-on-one interviews with adoption advocacy groups, target media, and some mainstream media. Finally, Jackson personally paid for full-page advertisements in the largest daily newspapers in several large cities (Boston, New York, Chicago, Dallas, and Los Angeles). The ads featured the foundation's new logo and were intended to make the foundation's presence known to those who might benefit from its adoption services, as well as those who might wish to make a donation. Similar advertising was planned in secondary markets over the next several months.

Internally, Jackson and the marketing team launched the new visual identity by meeting with all foundation employees to build excitement for the foundation's new adoption services, as well as about the new visual identity. Jackson talked about the history of the Spasiba Foundation and its mission of helping Russian orphans in Moscow. To reinforce the mission of the Spasiba Foundation as an organization that helps children both in Russia and in the United States, Jackson showed a video, set to music, that featured a montage of images of the children the foundation had helped, both those in Russia and those adopted by families in the United States. The video ended with an image of the foundation's new logo.

Case Discussion Questions

1. The purpose of a visual identity is to promote the organization in a consistent way, with the intent of promoting positive associations in the minds of the public. Discuss the specific visual identity issues this case illustrates. What are the implications of these issues?

2. Marketing employees at the Spasiba Foundation were experiencing frustration and confusion over the lack of a logo following the acquisition of the adoption agency and the announcement of a national launch for the foundation. If you were in charge,

how would you have communicated the delay in unveiling a new logo? Write a draft of your memo, e-mail, or speech, depending on the medium you chose.

3. Discuss the national launch of the Spasiba Foundation. What other tactics could Jennifer Jackson have used to promote the foundation's services to donors and prospective clients in the United States?

Bibliography

Allen, P.R. 1995. "Save Money with a Corporate Style Guide." *Technical Communication: Journal of the Society for Technical Communication* 42, no. 2: 284–289.

Blackburn, B. 1976. *Design Standards Manual: Their Meaning and Use for Federal Designers.* Washington, DC: National Endowment for the Arts.

Davis, J. 1996. *Advertising Research.* Upper Saddle River, NJ: Prentice-Hall.

Elliott, R. & N. Jankel-Elliott. 2003. "Using Ethnography in Strategic Consumer Research." *Qualitative Market Research: An International Journal* 6, no. 4: 215-223.

Frook, J.E. 2000. "Shell Goes Online for Global Brand Control." *B to B* (April 10): 51.

Holtzschue, L. 2006. *Understanding Color: An Introduction for Designers.* Hoboken, NJ: John Wiley & Sons.

Jeffries-Fox, B. 2003. "Advertising Value Equivalency (AVE)." Unpublished white paper sponsored by the Institute for Public Relations Commission on PR Measurement and Evaluation. Available at www.instituteforpr.org/research_single/adv_value_equiv/. Accessed March 5, 2008.

Krentzman, J. 1997. "Phil Knight: The Force Behind the Nike Empire." *Stanford Magazine*, January/February. Available at: www.stanfordalumni.org/news/magazine/1997/janfeb/articles/knight.html. Accessed April 15, 2009.

Krueger, R.A., and M.A. Casey. 2000. *Focus Groups: A Practical Guide for Applied Research.* 3rd ed. Thousand Oaks, CA: Sage Publications.

Leong, M. 2007. "It's the Ugly Games; Londoners Condemn the 2012 Olympics Logo as Hideous and Embarrassing." *National Post,* June 8, p. A3.

Lorge, S. 1998. "Better Off Branded." *Sales and Marketing Management* 150 (March): 39–42.

Murphy, K. 2007. "London's 2012 Olympic Logo Elicits Fits and Anger; Many Decry the Symbol as Ugly, and the Video Version Triggers Seizures." *Los Angeles Times,* June 8, p. A11.

Ogilvy PR Case Studies: LG Electronics. n.d. "LG Electronics Lights Up Times Square." Available at: www.ogilvypr.com/case-studies/lg-electronics.cfm. Accessed February 18, 2008.

Olins, W. and F. Selame. 1993. *The Corporate Identity Audit: A Set of Objective Measurement Tools for Your Company's Image and Reputation.* Zurich, Switzerland: Strategic Direction Publishers.

Peterson, B.L. 1996. *Using Design Basics to Get Creative Results.* Cincinnati: How Design Books.

Peterson, B.S. 2004. *Blue Streak: Inside jetBlue, the Upstart That Rocked an Industry.* New York: Penguin Group.

Phillips, P.L., and S.A. Greyser. 1999. *Creating a Corporate Identity for a $20 Billion Start-Up: Lucent Technologies.* Boston: Design Management Institute and Harvard Business School.

Rawsthorn, A. 2007. "Corporate Logos: Dynamic is the New Dynamic." *International Herald Tribune*, February 12, p. 10.

Sullivan, K. 2007. "Jeers and Loathing over a New Logo; Britons Denounce Olympics Symbol." *Washington Post*, June 4, p. C02.

truTV Web site. www.trutv.com/about/index.html.

"United Negro College Fund Revitalizes Its Brand." 2008. Available at www.reuters.com/article/pressRelease/idUS177452+17-Jan-2008+PRN20080117. Accessed February 18, 2008.

White, E. 2000. "Announcing Merger, But Not a Name, Costs Firms Plenty—Study Says That by Utilizing the Hot Media Spotlight Companies Gain Ad Value." *Wall Street Journal*, June 26, p. C24.

4

Changing an Existing Visual Identity

Monday, Monday . . .
Don't trust that day . . .
—The Mamas and the Papas

In June 2002, amid increased government oversight of the relationship between accounting firms' audit practices and their consulting arms, parent company PricewaterhouseCoopers announced that it was spinning off and renaming its consulting practice, PWC Consulting. On a Sunday, the new name was announced: Monday. According to press reports, PWC Consulting planned to spend $110 million—1.5 percent of the new firm's annual revenues—over the course of a year to promote and establish the new brand (Blakely 2002).

The announcement of the name change generated a mixed reaction on Internet message boards, and comments characterizing the name ranged from "whiny and ridiculous to funny and insightful. Some have solid arguments as to why the name is a shame; others contend that time will prove it's a stroke of genius" (Blakely 2002).

Time never became an issue. Within weeks, IBM entered into an agreement to buy Monday, killing the proposed name in the process.

This change in visual identity, although it never actually came to fruition, illustrates several important points, including the reasons *why* an established organization changes one or more elements of its visual identity, the extent of the change, the logistics of the promotion of the identity change, and public reaction to the change. These are four issues that any organization must consider.

Thinking Strategically About Visual Identity Changes: The Extent of the Change

Although there is only a nuanced difference between developing a new visual identity and changing an existing visual identity, since both require the development and launch of the visual identity itself, there are two important strategic questions concerning the change of an existing visual identity: why, or under what conditions, should an organization change its identity, and what should the extent of the change be? There are two types of changes associated with *any* visual identity: wholesale change and incremental change.

Wholesale Change

When an organization decides that its visual identity is not working because it is sending the wrong message—or not a strong enough message—it might decide to make a wholesale change in its identity: a complete overhaul of the name, logo, tagline, color palette, and so forth. This type of change is the most difficult on a strategic level as well as a logistical one.

Strategically speaking, changing an entire visual identity involves intense research on several fronts: why the identity needs to be changed, what the current identity reflects, what the new identity should reflect, and the intended consequence of changing the visual identity. Without very clear and specific answers to all of these questions—and perhaps more, depending upon the organization's unique circumstances—there should be no wholesale change of the identity. Making such a change when it is not warranted—and therefore not strategic—would be detrimental to the organization and its reputation.

Incremental Change

If an organization believes it needs an identity change, but not one that is a complete departure from its existing identity, it should choose one or more incremental changes. Might a name change, or a logo redesign, or even a new tagline more accurately reflect the associations the organization would like to conjure? If so, research could help to determine *which* element of the identity would help to best accomplish this change.

When Should a Visual Identity Change?

The decision to change an existing identity—or any individual identity elements—should not be made lightly. There is more to identity than meets the eye: rather than viewing the change as merely cosmetic, there must be discussions concerning the existing equity of the identity. Is the change going to be worthwhile in the long run? Some of the major reasons for visual identity changes are discussed below.

To Change Negative Associations

Negative associations with a visual identity can form in the public as a result of many things, including personal experience, organizational practices, or a widespread tragedy that makes it difficult to separate the identity of the organization with the tragedy itself.

Given the realities and repercussions of having a visual identity that conjures up negative associations, an organization should employ a strategy that aims to truly reflect the nature of the organization while also helping to build positive associations for it.

ValuJet Becomes AirTran

When ValuJet flight 592 crashed into the Everglades in May 1996, killing all of the passengers aboard, news reports focused on the advanced age of the fleet and the shoddy maintenance practices it employed. ValuJet was forced to shut down within weeks, grounding its fleet for three months until "serious deficiencies" could be corrected (Faiola and Phillips 1996).

In late 1997, however, ValuJet officially merged with AirTran, paying $61.8 billion for the airline and its name and visual identity. One branding expert agreed with the merger and the visual identity change and was quoted as saying: "If they are going to deliver any kind of service, they have to have reliability, quality and dependability. . . . They can't do that under the name of ValuJet—it's been devalued" ("Change of Name Best Way to Lose Identities of Past" 1997).

Ryder Trucks

When Timothy McVeigh detonated a Ryder truck full of explosives in front of the Alfred P. Murrah Federal Building in Oklahoma City on April 19, 1995, he killed 168 innocent victims. He also drew negative attention to Ryder trucks: nearly all news reports mentioned that the explosives had been contained in a Ryder truck rented by McVeigh. In the aftermath of the tragedy, Ryder had a difficult decision to make—change its name or the color of its trucks, or let time erase the negative associations cast upon Ryder by McVeigh's actions. Ryder chose the latter strategy, going about business as usual for many years. More recently, however, Ryder has changed its color palette, which included changing its fleet of vans and trucks from yellow to white.

Altria

Philip Morris has long been a corporate name associated with the manufacture and sale of tobacco products, most notably Marlboro brand cigarettes. While the company also owned and operated Kraft foods and Nabisco cookies, by and large it was associated with cigarettes.

In 2003, Philip Morris officially changed its corporate name to Altria and developed a rainbow-colored square logo made up of smaller, different-colored squares. The company kept the established Philip Morris name for its tobacco operations. According to corporate leaders, the company had evolved into far more than a tobacco company, so executives thought a new name would better reflect this diversity of product offerings ("Philip Morris Co. to Become Altria Group" 2001).

The Visual Identity Appears Outdated

Depending on the age of an organization, or even the design of its visual identity, elements of that visual identity can begin to appear outdated, or an organization's identity can appear confusing to some audiences. In the case of an outdated visual identity, an organization needs to think about how it is perceived: Does an outdated identity reflect a lack of innovation? Or does "outdated" actually genuinely reflect the image the organization would like to project? For example, a family business that has grown into a very large and financially successful company might maintain its seemingly "outdated" visual identity to preserve the feeling that it is small, as might be the case with Wegmans Food Markets.

Wegmans Food Markets, Inc.

In 2007, the Food Network honored Wegmans Food Markets with its "Super Market" award, calling the upstate New York–based family-owned chain of seventy-plus grocery stores the "grocery chain that has changed the way we shop." Wegmans is considered innovative in the grocery industry and is admired worldwide, having appeared on *Fortune* magazine's list of the "100 Best Companies to Work For" for a decade, and achieved the number one spot in 2005.

Even given all its national notoriety, Wegmans is still surprisingly "local" in its approach to visual identity. In fact, Wegmans' visual identity strategy seems to contradict the innovation for which the company has been honored. The stores, business practices, and Web site are innovative and cutting-edge, yet the company's logo and the exterior appearance of its stores are very dated, even old-fashioned.

To begin with, the exteriors of most Wegmans stores and Wegmans trucks, which are widely seen on the roadways transporting goods, are brown. In describing an older Wegmans store that was being replaced by a new one, a *Syracuse Post-Standard* reporter commented, "The old store has the dark-chocolate-color wood of the 1980s. The new store has the colonial brick of the . . . 1890s?" Andrea Walker of the *Baltimore Sun* described the company's corporate headquarters as "modest with an interior design reminiscent of the set of the 1960s *Brady Bunch* TV show" (2005). Similarly, the company's "Wegmans" logotype lettering has not changed in many years. As a result, it seems outdated in comparison to the company's many innovations in the industry, including in-store specialty shops, a variety of prepared foods, and its hiring of five-star professional chefs who offer in-store cooking demonstrations and gourmet cooking classes.

Part of the reason for this seemingly contradictory visual identity strategy may be Wegmans' attempts to maintain its public image as a small, local, family-owned grocery store even with its annual revenues reportedly exceeding $4 billion.

The Visual Identity Is Confusing

In the case of a confusing visual identity, it is in the organization's best interest to clear up the confusion, whether that involves changing the entire visual identity or just elements of it. The decision to engage in a change, however, needs to be strategic: minor "quick" fixes that ultimately do not change public perception are more detrimental in the long run than spending more time on firmly resolving the perception problem.

Syracuse University: From Interlocking SU to Block S

Syracuse University athletic director Daryl Gross was in his new job only a few months when he attended a meeting in New York City, to which he'd worn a logo jersey bearing the Syracuse University athletics logo, an interlocking SU that had been designed by Nike the year before. A fellow attendee looked at the logo and asked Gross if he was from St. John's University in New York City. From that point on, Gross began to realize that the Syracuse University athletics logo was not nationally recognized (personal communication 2005).

After just more than a year with the interlocking SU, Gross announced that the university's athletic program would be officially represented by a block S logo, one that had been used for decades but then was abandoned during the 1990s. Gross told the *Daily Orange*, the university's student newspaper, that the move back to the block S was not simply a marketing tactic, but part of a larger strategy he was implementing to attempt to "return the Orange to national prominence." Perhaps referring to the Nike-designed "Interlocking SU" logo, Gross commented: "We know it here intimately as SU, but outside of here people don't know SU. They do know when they see an orange 'S,' it's Syracuse. It's who we are."

Change to "Match" Existing Consumer Perceptions or Knowledge

Sometimes, brands enter the consciousness and quickly become part of the cultural lexicon, much like "Google" became a verb that refers to searching the Internet. Or, a company might change its corporate name to match its best-selling product or flagship store, such as when Dayton Hudson changed its name to Target Corporation in 2000 to reflect the success of its flagship store ("Company News" 2000).

In other cases, an organization or brand name becomes well known by the public, but under a shortcut or nickname, as was the case with FedEx. In these cases, the organization has the choice to keep its name as is, or change the visual identity to match.

FedEx Becomes a Verb

Federal Express was founded in 1971 and quickly became the national leader in overnight delivery services. Much like Google has become a verb for Internet searching, "FedEx" became a verb referring to overnight delivery. Instead of using Federal Express to send a package, people "FedEx" the package.

In the early 1990s, Federal Express made the strategic decision to change its visual identity to match consumer usage of its name. The organization adopted "FedEx" as its name, which was immediately recognizable to the public, but the company also needed to be concerned with the potential "genericide" of its name if the public began to use "FedEx" as a generic term for overnight delivery. (See Chapter 7 for a more thorough discussion of genericide and trademark abandonment.)

The FedEx logotype was designed by Landor Associates and over time appeared on the company's fleet of airplanes and trucks, as well as on all of the packaging materials used by organizations to ship millions of parcels. It soon became apparent that when you look closely at the FedEx logo, the white space between the "e" and "x" forms an arrow pointing to the right. Landor purposely designed the logo this way, but FedEx chose not to promote the arrow. Instead, the arrow, which connotes speed and precision, is considered a "hidden bonus."

The Law Tells You to Change Your Name: Andersen Consulting Becomes Accenture

Andersen Consulting was founded in 1989 as an affiliate of Andersen Worldwide, but in the summer of 2000 it was ordered by an independent arbitrator's ruling to change its name effective January 1, 2001. The name change was part of the consulting firm's desire to legally separate itself from its parent company, but also from the associations with its auditing practice, Arthur Andersen (which would later become embroiled in the Enron scandal).

In less than three months, Andersen Consulting's global marketing team worked with Landor Associates and law firms in 49 countries to develop and research a new name, including trademark searches on 3,000 names. It implemented BrandStorming, a firm-wide program for its 65,000 employees to submit ideas for a new name. More than 2,677 names were submitted from 42 countries, "Accenture" included.

On January 1, 2001, Accenture officially launched its new name with a variety of marketing communications to alert the public and new office signage and stationery to alert employees. The name reportedly reflected the company's "accent" on the future, but more skeptical naming experts speculated that the first three letters of the new name are meant to be reflective of the Andersen Consulting Company acronym ("Andersen Consulting Announces New Name—Accenture—Effective 01.01.01" 2000).

To Streamline a Parent Organization and Affiliates

There are many parent organizations that have local affiliates, particularly clubs with a national headquarters and regional chapters. The parent organization can either dictate a branding strategy that aligns the national organization with its affiliates, or the parent organization can allow the local affiliates to brand themselves using visual identities developed on the local level, without illustrating a specific connection to the parent organization.

Regardless of the initial branding strategy, there are often circumstances that dictate a change in strategy that requires streamlining the organizations to have a unified look. In this case, each of the local affiliates must adopt a new visual identity that aligns it with the parent organization.

American Advertising Federation

The American Advertising Federation (AAF), the "unifying voice for advertising," is a national nonprofit trade organization made up of 200 local advertising clubs as well as 215 college chapters across the country. For years, the AAF did not dictate a particular branding strategy for its local chapters, and names across the country typically contained the term "advertising club" along with the city or state name, but generally they did not include any reference to the AAF.

In 2007, the AAF announced that it was requesting that its local chapters adopt a specific branding strategy that requires each chapter to adopt the American Advertising Federation as its name, with a smaller reference to the chapter's location. For example, the Syracuse Ad Club became "American Advertising Federation—Syracuse."

The AAF announced that the new visual identity strategy "reflects a nationwide shift in clubs across the country to be more readily identified as part of the larger American Advertising Federation (AAF). . . . The new brand makes you a national organization with national connections. . . . Merging our identity expands your recognition and reputation throughout the country while retaining your hometown roots . . . That's what being part of the AAF family means. . . . That's the power of unifying the brand" ("We've Changed Our Name" 2007).

To Spur Sales of Licensed Products

There are many types of organizations that sell logo merchandise to the public, and depending on the audience, a change in a visual identity—and therefore new apparel—might spur sales and generate revenue.

Those in the sports industry profit greatly from the sale of products and apparel bearing a team's name, logo, and signature colors. This type of arrangement is called a trademark licensing arrangement, whereby an organization (in this case a sports team) grants permission for an apparel maker to produce a product bearing the identity elements. The apparel maker typically pays for the license itself and guarantees the team a percentage of royalties on each product sold.

In the case of the highly profitable collegiate licensing industry, universities can employ the services of Collegiate Licensing Company, an Atlanta-based organization that manages the application and actual licensing process for more than 200 colleges and universities, as well as specific events such as football bowl games, organizations such as the NCAA and its athletic conferences, and the Heisman Trophy (Collegiate Licensing Company, www.clc.com).

Colleges and universities typically receive a royalty of approximately 10 percent on each item sold. Stop to consider the revenue potential for a licensing agreement with a large university: The University of North Carolina at Chapel Hill has an enrollment of approximately 27,000 undergraduate and graduate students at any given time, plus a living alumni population of more than 210,000. In addition, the University of North Carolina men's basketball team captured the national championship title in 2005, spurring sales of logo merchandise. In fact, between 2001 and 2005, the University of North Carolina was the number-one seller of logo merchandise, and the university received 10 percent of the cost of each item.

It is not unreasonable to assume that the loyalty of the UNC fans could induce them to buy new apparel featuring a newly developed logo or color palette, which may account for the trend in the collegiate apparel market to produce college merchandise outside the school's typical color palette (pink Syracuse hats, for example, when the university's signature color is orange).

This practice is not simply part of the collegiate apparel market, however. Professional sports teams routinely issue new apparel in an attempt to increase sales. In the case of the Washington Capitols, a National Hockey League franchise, the organization reissued its uniform to match its inaugural one, partly in an attempt to sell more merchandise. The team's marketing officer remarked: "We want fans walking around wearing our stuff. It raises our brand awareness and that helps us create more fans" (El-Bashir 2007, p. E01).

The Logistics of Promoting a Visual Identity Change

Regardless of the reason a visual identity is changed, there are a number of logistical issues that need to be considered. The first consideration is the question of who will actually execute the redesign. For example, will the organization charge an in-house team with developing a new identity, or will it hire an external consultant or agency to manage the process? This is a question that can be answered only by knowing the project's budget, timeline, and myriad other variables that are particular to the organization. While expensive, and perhaps prohibitively so for some small organizations, the cost of hiring an identity firm needs to be viewed in the context of its expertise and resources: these specialized firms have an intimate knowledge of the visual identity development process as well as the resources to conduct the appropriate types of research. Working in tandem with the organization itself, visual identity firms can provide invaluable expertise in a visual identity redesign process.

Once the new visual identity is developed, chief among the organization's concerns should be the timing of the press announcement. When Syracuse University changed its visual identity, its own announcement was trumped by the press, so the university did not have the opportunity to address the change as it had wanted. When undergoing a visual identity change of any kind, it is important for the organization to remain in control as much as possible. Retaining control enables the organization to unveil the identity on its own schedule, and to provide the message it desires—rather than to be blindsided by the press announcement and have the organization's message dictated by the media.

When FedEx underwent its visual identity transformation, the process took two years and was done secretly, which is not unusual for high-profile organizations. The interesting part of the FedEx visual identity story is the "legend" that has grown up around it:

> Under a cloak of secrecy on June 22, 1994, a mysterious aircraft landed on a darkened runway in Memphis and was swiftly guided into an awaiting hangar. Only a handful of security guards standing watch against intruders witnessed the late night operation, which took less than 20 minutes to complete. Two days later the whole world knew the secret. With news media, public officials and 4,000 FedEx employees present (and another 100,000 employees watching the event on the company's private FX-TV), the world's largest overnight delivery carrier unveiled its new corporate

identity—the culmination of two years of research and design and weeks of clandestine implementation. Video relays around the globe carried an event that usually doesn't get much play beyond a company's in-house newsletter. (Corporate Design Foundation n.d.)

Once the new visual identity has been developed, the true logistics of the change process come into play. When a change to a visual identity is made, however small, everything that bore any or all elements of the previous visual identity needs to be destroyed and then replaced with the new visual identity.

When the Washington Capitols changed their visual identity, the organization was forced to change dozens of items, "from player underwear to locker name plates to travel bags to all 1,500 hours of video played on the monitors during home games" (El-Bashir 2007, p. E01).

Although every organization will have specific needs and items that need to be addressed, the Appendix features a checklist of many of the items that typically contain one or more elements of an organization's visual identity (Gregory and Wiechmann 1999). It is best not to wait until the redesign is complete to begin thinking about how to implement the new visual identity. Rather, during the process, the organization should determine whether it is best served by a clean sweep or rollout strategy.

Clean Sweep

A clean sweep strategy is the more dramatic implementation option, whereby organizations destroy everything that contains the former visual identity and then immediately replace those items with items containing the new visual identity—all of which are ready the day of the visual identity launch and press announcement.

The clean sweep strategy ensures a quick and seamless implementation, but it also requires a tremendous financial investment and impeccable attention to detail. For these reasons, it is typically only the most well-funded and sophisticated organizations that are able to fully pursue this implementation strategy. More likely, given inevitable financial and time constraints, organizations will choose a rollout strategy.

Rollout

In this context, a rollout strategy refers to the gradual implementation (and replacement) of the new visual identity across all media—architecture and organizational literature, stationery, apparel, and so on—that will bear the new visual identity. This type of strategy allows organizations to make gradual investments in all of their new visual identity touchpoints, but it also means that organizations risk having two versions of their visual identity in front of the public.

Gradual investments in new visual identity touchpoints are more of a concern for those organizations with a limited budget for the implementation. For example, new business cards and letterhead are low-cost items during the transition to the new visual identity, but building signage and interior designs present relatively high costs within a limited budget.

If employing a rollout strategy, the organization needs to determine a timeline for investments in the new touchpoints, and which touchpoints are most important to unveil at the time of the new visual identity launch. For example, is a major investment in building signage worth it if it is not imperative that the general public be made aware of the change immediately? If the organization is a charity, perhaps a letter—on new letterhead—to contributors and donors alerting them to the change is a wiser investment in the short term, and larger investments can be made over time.

Regardless of the duration of the rollout, organizations need to enter into this type of strategy with a timeline for the process (even if the process is expected to take three to five years). Scheduling the major changes, such as exterior signage and vehicle fleet changes, over a number of years will help to coordinate the change process, as well as provide some sense of budget needs in the years after the initial visual identity launch (Olins and Selame 1993).

Public Reaction to Visual Identity Changes

Regardless of the organization's reason for changing its visual identity, or the strategy it chooses to implement the new identity, one thing any organization can count on is public reaction to the new visual identity. Depending on the size and stature of the organization, public opinion could be played out in a small way through word-of-mouth among a tiny, tight-knit community of stakeholders, or it could play out in a large way through the national media and internationally on blogs and other social media. For this reason, it should be the goal of every organization that undergoes a visual identity change to explain to its stakeholders and the public *why* the change took place.

Another type of public response that publicly traded firms need to consider is the reaction of the stock market itself: while a name change in and of itself might not have a substantive effect, it could signal to the market that larger changes are taking place at the firm (Horsky and Swyngedouw 1987).

Below are three examples of two visual identity changes that illustrate some of the reasons why organizations have changed elements of their visual identities, and how the public has reacted to them.

Altria

When Philip Morris officially changed its corporate name to Altria in 2003, it announced that "Altria" was "derived from the Latin word 'altus' [high], and conveys the notion of 'reaching ever higher'" (Martin, 2007). Altria was referring to its performance, both financially and with respect to the quality of its products. The choice of Altria—and highlighting its supposed Latin root—seems ironic in the context of why Philip Morris changed its name, which was to highlight its nontobacco products.

This corporate name change garnered mixed reaction from stakeholder groups, from stock analysts to antismoking advocacy groups. An analyst with Salomon Smith Barney highlighted the fact that a name change does not solve all of an organization's problems:

> The fact that they're changing the name suggests they believe there's a negative associated with the name. I don't believe there's any negative associated with the name. . . . I think the difficulties the company faces are on the litigation and public policy front and I don't think the change of name is going to make any difference. ("Philip Morris Co. to become Altria Group" 2001)

An analyst from Morgan Stanley Dean Witter, however, believed the name change would help diminish negative associations: "It's hard to make an argument you're more than a tobacco company when you have a name people associate with tobacco" ("Philip Morris Co. to become Altria Group" 2001).

And as executives at Philip Morris most likely expected, antitobacco groups felt the name change was an attempt to deflect attention from the company's focus on manufacturing cigarettes. The Campaign for Tobacco-Free Kids said the name change would not alter the company's association with cigarettes. "Philip Morris is changing its name because it is unwilling to change its harmful business practices" ("Philip Morris Co. to become Altria Group" 2001).

Syracuse University

Reaction among Syracuse University students to its athletic teams' name from "Orangemen" to the more simple and nongendered "The Orange" was not immediate, given the timing of the athletic department's announcement shortly after students had left campus for the summer. Once they returned to campus for the fall 2004 semester, however, students reacted strongly and were vocal about the timing of the announcement.

Many students wondered why the announcement of the new visual identity was made after most students had already left campus for the summer. The university's athletic director subsequently explained that the timing of the announcement was his "sole regret" in the process. He explained that the intention was to make the announcement several weeks later, with a coordinated message going out to alumni, students, and other fans. It seems the media broke the story before the athletic department was ready ("Jake's Take: SU's Athletics Logo" 2004).

Public reaction was strong and swift: an Internet petition addressed to the athletic department had more than 5,000 signatories within three months. Those signing the petition claimed that "any change to (the) nicknames—even to 'Orange'—would cause irreparable harm to [their] allegiance, loyalty, passion and support for Syracuse University and its athletic teams" (Janela 2004).

Those who signed the petition were quite vocal about the change, and many begged the administration to reconsider changing the name of the athletic teams. It was clear from reading the petitioners' comments that the athletic director's explanation of what "The Orange" meant had not been fully accepted by the general public. One petitioner understood the reason for the change, but questioned the new nickname: "While I'm sure SU meant for the title of 'The Orange' to unite the student body under one name and render us as a fearless bunch like a name such as 'The Crimson Tide,' the mental picture of a gigantic orange rolling down a city street does not strike terror into my heart but rather makes me laugh."

Some sportswriters also took a humorous approach to covering the university's transformation from "Orangemen" and "Orangewomen" to "The Orange." From an article in *Sports Illustrated:* "Great marketing strategy.

Why be represented by some cute, innocuous mascot when you can be associated with a threat level on the terror alert chart?" (Scheft 2004).

Legal Issues Related to Visual Identity Changes

Regardless of why, how, or when an organization changes its visual identity, there are legal issues that need to be addressed before, during, and after the change process.

Trademark issues should be the primary legal consideration before embarking on a visual identity change of any kind. Specifically, names and designs that are potential new identity elements should be considered only after determining that they are available as trademarks. Once it is determined that the chosen name or design are available as trademarks, it is imperative that the organization begin its own trademark registration process. Trademark issues are discussed in greater detail in Chapter 7.

Other legal issues to consider during and after the visual identity development process include copyright issues, which may come into play once the identity is promoted. Copyright issues are discussed in greater detail in Chapter 8.

Finally, to ensure that the organization is in control of its visual identity and is able to reap the benefits of having developed it, the organization needs to consider incorporating any new organizational names, if appropriate. The first step in ensuring the success of a visual identity is ensuring that the organization understands how to properly protect the identity from infringement.

Summary

The decision to change an existing identity—or any individual identity elements—should not be made lightly. Rather than viewing even minor changes as merely cosmetic, there must be discussions concerning the existing equity of the identity and the strategy behind changing it.

There are a number of considerations when an established organization changes one or more elements of its visual identity, including: the extent of the change (should the change be wholesale or incremental?), the logistics of the promotion of the identity change (should it be a rollout or a clean sweep strategy?), and most importantly, why the visual identity should change—to change negative associations, to change an outdated visual identity, to change a confusing visual identity, to "match" existing perceptions, to streamline a parent organization with its affiliates, to spur sales of a product, or because the law tells the organization to change? In any of the above cases, the organization should be aware of—and ready to accept—the public's reaction to the change.

Additional issues to consider when changing a visual identity include the communication of the visual identity change itself: which stakeholders should be receiving the message? How should the message be sent? Finally, organizations need to consider early on the legal issues associated with the visual identity change, both before, during and after the change occurs. Trademark and copyright issues, as well as issues of incorporation, will help the organization to retain control of the visual identity.

Case Study: Cycle Challenge Changes Its Name

Cycle Challenge, Inc., was a nonprofit organization whose sole mission was to organize and host Cycle Challenge, an annual 300-mile, 6-day bicycle ride that raised money for the homeless around New England. The ride's route was mapped out to showcase the most beautiful natural landmarks New England offered. As a result, ride organizers had hoped to attract a number of serious riders, but also families interested in using the ride as a family vacation. After its first year, however, organizers looked at the disappointing turnout and wondered how to achieve the goal of attracting more amateur riders.

In its inaugural year, Cycle Challenge had attracted just 76 riders, each having raised $300 in pledges as a requirement for entry. The $22,800 raised barely covered the cost of the ride logistics, which included food and overnight accommodations for the riders, as well as the required medical staff.

Costs for the ride itself were quite reduced for Cycle Challenge, since the organization maintained close ties with many of New England's large companies and philanthropic residents, many of whom donated resources and funding for the ride. In return for this consideration, Cycle Challenge felt a responsibility to consult its benefactors on its major strategic decisions.

When ride organizers met on a Monday morning several weeks after the ride, it was to brainstorm ideas on how to attract more riders and therefore raise more money for their cause: the homeless. Many on the Cycle Challenge staff felt that simply promoting the ride earlier in the season would help to attract more riders. With a June ride date, Cycle

Challenge had started promoting the ride right after the first of the year. They believed promoting the ride beginning in September to recruit riders for the following June would help.

Some on the Cycle Challenge staff felt there were strategic changes that could affect the organization's ability to attract riders while also better promoting the cause. As it was, the name Cycle Challenge sounded more daunting than the ride was, and many felt it was scaring potential riders away, particularly the families the organization was trying to attract. One staff member, who also had completed the ride, suggested that the ride's intense name was not reflective of what the ride actually was—an almost leisurely bike tour that allowed riders to get some exercise while taking in tourist attractions and also helping the homeless.

Some staff members were hesitant about changing the name of the bike ride, but others on the Cycle Challenge staff began to see changing the ride's name as a positive step toward achieving the organization's goals. After much discussion, the staff voted to change the name of the bike ride, but there was no clear decision about what to name it. Staff suggested tactics like naming contests and brainstorm sessions, but the executive director suggested hiring a visual identity firm.

Because the cost of hiring a visual identity firm would have wiped out Cycle Challenge's annual budget, the executive director approached the organization's largest corporate benefactor, a Boston-based office supply goods company, to ask the company to fund the cost of the name change. During the meeting, the CEO of the supply goods company asked several questions that Cycle Challenge's executive director could not answer: What was the timeline for the change, the budget, and how would Cycle Challenge deal with a name change while also planning next year's charity ride? In the end, however, the CEO agreed to fund the cost of the name change on the condition that the new name truly reflected the nature of the bike ride.

Once the visual identity firm was hired, a core group of three Cycle Challenge staff devoted their time exclusively to working with the firm on the name change. The staff members were invaluable in helping the visual identity firm understand the organization and the bike ride. Also, assigning staff members to the name change project meant that the entire name change team could complete the ride in the course of its research. This type of first-hand knowledge of the route and the landmarks was invaluable in naming the ride.

After approximately one month of intensive research that included the bike ride, interviews with riders from the inaugural Cycle Challenge, and surveys of potential riders (from a list of e-mail addresses provided by the organization), the visual identity firm presented three potential names to the staff at Cycle Challenge: New England Shelter Ride, Cycle for Shelter, and Riding for Rooms. The staff overwhelmingly dismissed the last choice, since they did not think it was as serious a name as the ride deserved given the charity it supported. The two remaining names were given serious consideration, with the staff pretty well divided on the final decision.

Case Discussion Questions

1. How would you characterize the type of change Cycle Challenge was making to its organizational visual identity? Was the change justified, in your opinion?
2. With a staff divided on the remaining name choices, how should the organization proceed with selecting a new name?
3. Cycle Challenge has a limited promotions budget. If you were in charge of marketing for the nonprofit organization, what would be your approach to promoting the new name? What type of marketing tactics would you employ?

Bibliography

Altria Web site. www.altria.com.
"Andersen Consulting Announces New Name—Accenture—Effective 01.01.01." 2000. Press release by Andersen Consulting. Available at http://newsroom. accenture.com/article_display.cfm?article_id=4170. Accessed April 22, 2008.
Blakely, B. 2002. "Monday: PwC Consulting's New Name Creates Controversy, Cackles." TechRepublic, July 17. Available at http://articles.techrepublic.com. com/5100–6333–1038748.html. Accessed April 14, 2008.
"Change of Name Best Way to Lose Identities of Past: ValuJet Latest to Dump Old Moniker." 1997. *San Antonio Express-News*, July 11, p. 1E.
Collegiate Licensing Company Web site. www.clc.com.
"Company News; Dayton Hudson Says It Will Change Its Name to Target." 2000. *New York Times*, January 14. Available online at www.nytimes.com. Accessed April 21, 2009.
Corporate Design Foundation. n.d."Why Federal Express Became FedEx." @*issue*. Available at www.cdf.org/issue_journal/why_federal_express_became_fedex. html. Accessed April 14, 2008.
El-Bashir, T. 2007. "Back in Red, White and Blue, Caps Make a Colorful Statement." *Washington Post,* June 22, p. E01.

Faiola, A., and D. Phillips. 1996. "ValuJet Agrees to Shut Down; FAA Cites 'Serious Deficiencies'; Agency Shakeup Near, Sources Say." *Washington Post*, June 18, p. A01.

Gregory, J.R., and J.G. Wiechmann. 1999. *Marketing Corporate Image: The Company as Your Number One Product.* Chicago: NTC Business Books.

Horsky, D., and P. Swyngedouw. 1987. "Does It Pay to Change Your Company's Name? A Stock Market Perspective." *Marketing Science* 6, no. 4: 320–335.

"Jake's Take: SU's Athletics Logo." 2004. Available at www.suathletics.com/news/Football/2004/5/14/jakestakeLOGO.asp. Accessed May 4, 2009.

Janela, M. 2004. "New Orange Logo, Nickname Incites Controversy." *Daily Orange*, August 30. Available at www.media.www.dailyorange.com. Accessed April 21, 2009.

Martin, A. 2007. "Altria Board To Consider A Spinoff Overseas." *New York Times,* August 25. Available at www.nytimes.com/2007/08/25/business/worldbusiness/25altria.html. Accessed May 5, 2009.

Olins, W. and E. Selame. 1993. *The Corporate Identity Audit: A Set of Objective Measurement Tools for Your Company's Image and Reputation.* Zurich, Switzerland: Strategic Direction Publishers.

"Philip Morris Co. to become Altria Group." 2001. *Modern Brewery Age.* November 26.

Portugal, J., and K.D. Halloran. 1986. "Avoiding a Corporate Identity Crisis." *Management Review* 75, no. 4, 43–45.

Scheft, B. 2004. "The Show: Syracuse Changes Nickname from Orangemen to Orange." *Sports Illustrated*, May 24.

"Syracuse Officially Changes to Orange." 2004. *Rochester Democrat and Chronicle,* May 12.

Walker, Andrea. 2005. "Upscale Wegmans Supermarkets Becomes a 'Major Draw' in Communities." *Baltimore Sun*, September 25.

"We've Changed Our Name." 2007. *AAF–Fort Worth News.* Available at http://fwadclub.wordpress.com/category/local-news/. Accessed April 22, 2008.

Part 2

Protection of Visual Identity

5

Research as Protection

Visual Identity Audits

> *Different audiences will form a view of an organization based on the*
> *totality of the impressions that the company makes on them. When*
> *these impressions are contradictory—where the impressions made in*
> *one place are different from those made somewhere else—the overall*
> *impressions will be confusing at best and negative at worst.*
> —Wally Olins and Elinor Selame (1993)

Just as research is a necessary tool in the development of an organization's visual identity, it can also provide an opportunity to review—and in some cases, protect—the larger, mass effects of the visual identity. This type of primary research is referred to as a visual identity audit. By taking a comprehensive view of the ways in which the visual identity is projected to stakeholders and also perceived by them, a visual identity audit helps an organization to more fully understand the internal and external environments in which its visual identity exists.

Schmitt and Simonson provide an eloquent statement on the rationale behind conducting a visual identity audit in a corporate context:

> Managers usually want an assessment of the current state of aesthetics or identity in their own company relative to its competition. This assessment entails discovering "who we are" in terms of our aesthetic presence. While this kind of inquiry might sound mystical or hokey, it can actually be quite rigorous and systematic. It involves a straightforward company, customer and competitive analysis and a consideration of broader cultural factors that impact customer tastes and preferences. (1997, p. 196)

Visual Identity Audits Defined

A visual identity audit is twofold: it is a comprehensive look at the organization's visual identity elements as well as a measure of the perception of those elements and the organization in the minds of its relevant stakeholders. The audit is a collection of images reflecting the projection of an organization's visual identity, followed by a series of interviews with members of both internal and external publics that are important to the organization and its success. The audit is meant to be a comprehensive look at how an organization's visual identity is presented in the marketplace, but just as importantly, conducting a thorough visual identity audit can help to address gaps in perception across the organization's stakeholders.

The Visual Identity Audit Process

In order to conduct a valuable visual identity audit, the organization must have the consent, approval, and "buy-in" of senior management, preferably the CEO or highest-level manager of the organization. The process of planning and conducting a visual identity audit is discussed in more detail below, with a more in-depth look at the two major components of a visual identity audit: image collection and analysis, and audit interviews.

Olins and Selame (1993) write extensively on visual identity audits as a management tool. They contend that the first decision that must be made is whether the organization should hire an outside agency to conduct the audit. For some organizations, this might be cost prohibitive, but for others it could provide a much-needed objective third-party opinion. In either case, Olins and Selame outline a process that begins with selecting the best visual identity audit team.

Selecting the Audit Team

The selection of the right employees for the visual identity audit team is the first—and perhaps the most important—decision the organization must make. Senior managers should ensure that the team has the respect that it will take to get other employees involved in the audit process. First and foremost, the team should include a graphic designer. Olins and Selame (1993) also believe the team must be cross-functional: members should hail from every department in the organization—from sales and marketing to operations and engineering. This will ensure that every facet of the organization is represented in the visual identity discussion.

Writing the Audit Brief

The first task for the audit team is to write the audit brief. Because an effective and valuable visual identity audit will be a comprehensive view of the visual identity's projection and perception, it will undoubtedly involve people and departments within the organization that are not typically involved in the day-to-day promotion or protection of the identity. For this reason, each member of the organization should be made aware of the visual identity audit through the audit brief, which ensures that everyone understands the purpose of the audit as well as the process. The brief also serves to keep the audit team focused during the audit process.

The audit brief should be written by the audit team, but also approved by senior management:

> [The brief] should be comprehensive and take into account [the audit's] parameters in terms of strategy, marketing, communication and behavior. A short version of this brief should be circulated to senior and middle management who will, where appropriate, cascade it down to their own departments. A variation should also be circulated to selected external audiences. (Olins and Selame 1993, p. 15)

Olins and Selame suggest that an audit brief should be comprehensive, but also simple to understand and succinctly written:

> We are currently examining how clearly the activities of the company and its component parts are understood by our own staff and by those with whom we come into contact, such as suppliers, customers, financial audiences and so on. Because of this concern, I have asked a small team to explore the issue. If any member of the team contacts you, I would be grateful if you would give them your co-operation. Naturally, all discussions will be confidential. (1993, p. 15)

Collecting and Analyzing Touchpoints

Since the essence of a visual identity is rooted in its design, the first substantive step in a visual identity audit entails collecting as many internal and external touchpoints as possible that contain elements of the visual identity—everything from letterhead to national advertising. The audit team should also visit and photograph the exterior and interiors of build-ings, retail and wholesale stores, offices, and any other architecture that reflects elements of the visual identity. Napoles (1988) writes:

> An important ingredient in our conceptual and creative problem-solving methods as designers is to understand the environment—external and internal—in which the design and the subsequent communications system must work. The team will visit, photograph, and analyze Widget's regional offices, plus three to four principal competitive offices. We will also audit a selection of printed items with Widget's current identity: letterhead, forms, business cards, brochures, and so forth.

When Pepsi wanted to learn how consistently its visual identity ele-ments were being projected to consumers around the world, it hired Landor Associates to perform a visual identity audit. The agency col-lected 2,000 photographs of Pepsi identity elements (in this case the name and logo as it was used on signage and on soda cans) from thirty-four countries (Quelch 1998).

Once the touchpoints have been collected, it is integral to the audit process that the team analyze the touchpoints for consistency. If the or-ganization has several chapters or divisions, is each of them projecting the visual identity the same way? Are employees in different states or different countries projecting the visual identity the same way? These questions can be answered very easily with a thorough analysis of the touchpoints. To achieve a broad view of the touchpoints, it is advisable to choose a room and "wallpaper" it with the images. Once they are hanging close together, inconsistencies become apparent very quickly and easily.

What Pepsi's audit team found in its analysis of its touchpoints was startling: there were a number of inconsistencies in the identity elements being used both within some countries and between countries. Also, there was no one color that was singularly associated with Pepsi, since it had used red, white, and blue for much of its history (in comparison to Coca-Cola, which has strong associations with the color red) (Quelch 1998).

The visual identity touchpoints provide information for the interview phase of the audit, and collecting the touchpoints early provides the team with enough time to analyze the results and develop questions based on the content of the touchpoints themselves or any inconsistencies uncovered.

Table 5.1

Internal and External Stakeholders

Internal Stakeholders	External Stakeholders
All staff	Customers
Board of directors	Investment analysts
Investors	Stockbrokers
Retirees	Opinion leaders
Union representatives	Media
Families of employees	Suppliers
	Competitors
	Government regulatory agencies
	Nongovernmental organizations (NGOs)
	Local community
	Trade organizations
	Recruiters and potential recruits

Conducting Audit Interviews

During the image collection and analysis phase of the visual identity audit, the focus is on ensuring that the identity is *projected* in a consistent way. Once the touchpoints have been thoroughly analyzed, the visual identity audit moves onto the follow-up interview phase, during which the focus is on ensuring that the visual identity is *perceived* in the way the organization intended.

To prepare for the interview phase of the visual identity audit, the audit team should carefully consider who is to be interviewed. Both internal and external stakeholders who can lend insight into the visual identity should be interviewed. Table 5.1 provides a list of the people who should be considered for interviews, according to Olins and Selame (1993).

The audit interviews with both internal and external stakeholders typically focus on four areas of organizational visual identity: the organization's products or services, environments in which the visual identity is projected, the organization's communications, and the behavior of the organization (Olins and Selame 1993).

Generally speaking, Olins and Selame (1993) write, the interviews are intended to find out how much the interview subjects know about the organization, what clear and consistent opinions they have of it, and how far those opinions diverge from the identity the organization believes it is projecting through its visual identity. In order to achieve the depth required to achieve these results, Olins and Selame (1993) suggest 30

Figure 5.1
Suggested Questions for the Internal Visual
Identity Audit Interview

1. How long have you been with the organization? Where did you work before you worked here?
2. What is your position/responsibility in the organization?
3. Have your perceptions of the organization changed since you became affiliated with it? What were your perceptions before? What are they now?
4. What image attributes (characteristics) do you associate with your organization?
5. How would you describe your organization and its products/services to someone who asked?
6. In your opinion, is your organization understood by outsiders as you understand it? If not, how do outsiders view the organization?
7. Who do you believe are your organization's major competitors?
8. Where do you see the organization's opportunities for growth?
9. What barriers are preventing the organization from achieving this growth?
10. What is your opinion of the current visual identity used by the organization?
11. What does the current symbol/signature/trademark suggest to you? Do you think it reflects the personality and long-term mission of the organization?
12. What colors do you associate with the organization?
13. What are the major strengths and weaknesses of the organization?
14. What are the major strengths and weaknesses of the organization's products/services?
15. In what ways do you think the organization could communicate better to its diverse publics?
16. Is the organization known mainly through its organizational name, or its product or service brand names?
17. How does the organization articulate the relationship between brand names and the organization's name?

Source: Olins and Selame (1993).

Figure 5.2
Suggested Questions for the External Visual Identity Audit Interview

1. What is your relationship to the organization?
2. How familiar would you say you are with the organization? (Prompt: very familiar, somewhat familiar, not at all familiar)
3. How would describe what the organization does? What specific brand name products/services does it offer?
4. Do you believe the organization is a regional, national, or international organization?
5. Who do you believe are the organization's primary competitors?
6. Based on what you know, have heard, or have read, would you rate the organization's reputation as excellent, good, fair, or poor?
7. When you hear [the organization's name], what things come to mind?
8. Why do you do business with the organization?
9. Would you recommend this organization's products/services to a friend?
10. Can you recall or describe any advertising the organization has done recently? How did it influence your perception of the organization?
11. What symbol and colors come to mind when you hear the organization's name?
12. What image attributes (characteristics) do you associate with the organization?
13. How would you rate this organization's products/services on a scale of one to five when compared to the competition?
14. How would you rate the organization's literature in presenting an identity that is clear and consistent with organization's desired positioning?
15. Is the organization well positioned/badly positioned in the market place?
16. How big is the organization's share of the market? How profitable is it?
17. How many people does the organization employ?

(continued)

Figure 5.2 *(continued)*

18. Who are its main competitors?
19. What is the long-term vision of the organization? In your opinion, will the organization's management have the ability to execute the vision?
20. Generally speaking, has the organization improved or deteriorated in the last five years?
21. Is there an admired organizational model within the industry? If so, which organization is it? What makes it the admired model?
22. How is it better/worse than this organization?
23. Is the organization known mainly through its organizational name or through its product or service brand names?
24. How does the organization articulate the relationship between brand names and the organization's name?

Source: Olins and Selame (1993).

interviews of key internal stakeholders and 30 key external stakeholders, each lasting between 30 and 60 minutes. Based on their work, Figure 5.1 includes a suggested list of questions for the internal interview, and Figure 5.2 includes a suggested list for the external interview. Both sets of questions are adapted from Olins and Selame (1993).

The FedEx Approach

In the early 1990s, overnight shipping giant Federal Express decided that its visual identity needed a change. Instead of choosing to conduct its visual identity audit in-house, it decided to hire Landor Associates, a leading visual identity agency.

> "We were asked to take a good hard look at the company and its markets, assess Federal Express's position, and make any needed adjustments," says Lindon Leader, senior design director at Landor. Over the next year, Landor's research unit conducted some 40 focus groups with employees and customers and interviewed industry leaders in 12 markets around the

world. It also compared Federal Express's existing identity with the identities of a range of technology-smart companies known for innovation and marketing savvy. ("Why Federal Express Became FedEx" n.d.)

Research conducted by Landor found that Federal Express had a tremendous amount of brand equity. Surprisingly, however, the shorter form of the company's name, FedEx, which had become a verb, had the same equity. Landor found that both names were associated with speed, reliability, innovation, and customer service. The name Federal Express, however, also had negative connotations:

> In 1973, the word had given the company immediate equity, an official alternative to the post office, but today it was more often associated with being bureaucratic and slow. In Latin American countries, it conjured images of the *federales*, and in some other parts of the world, people had trouble pronouncing Federal Express. ("Why Federal Express Became FedEx" n.d.)

Using the Audit Results

When the audit is complete, a thorough analysis of the data will likely yield one of two results: The organization might be evaluated as consistently projecting an identity that is positively perceived by the public, in which case it should continue with its visual identity program. More likely, the audit results will show that the organization has some work to do to achieve a truly consistent presentation of its visual identity among its many audiences.

Before embarking on a large-scale change in promotion tactics, however, the organization should carefully consider any inconsistencies. Significant differences between promotional materials are important to note, but the organization should consider the audiences for the materials: if more than one kind of material is seen by the same audience, changes will definitely need to be made. If the two sets of materials are never seen by the same audience, then the inconsistencies will be less noticeable and can therefore be changed over time (Olins and Selame 1993).

Whatever the outcome, because the decision to conduct a visual identity audit is often made only after serious deliberation, the organization should have a plan for how it will use the results of the audit. For some organizations, the audit might be a precursor to a definite visual identity change. In this case, the audit results would be used to help define the new identity elements. For other organizations, the audit might be intended as a benchmark to determine how consistently the organization has projected its identity to its various audiences, and also how positively the visual identity is perceived by those audiences.

Regardless of the organization-specific uses of the audit data, just the simple fact of having conducted the visual identity audit could be valuable. If the organization is ever in a position to have to defend the use of its visual identity in the course of trademark litigation, the audit data serve as a benchmark on the strength of the visual identity. Should such a situation arise, preemptive evidence gathered from an audit is typically an unbiased measure of pre- and post-effects of the organization's promotion efforts. Also, if the organization's efforts to stop trademark infringement wind up being carried out in the legal arena, surveys may be helpful in obtaining a preliminary injunction early in the proceedings.

Summary

A visual identity audit is a comprehensive look at the organization's visual identity elements as well as a measure of the perception of those elements and the organization in the minds of its relevant stakeholders. The audit consists of the collection of images reflecting the projection of the organization's visual identity, followed by a series of interviews with members of both internal and external publics. The visual identity audit process includes selecting the audit team, writing the audit brief, collecting and analyzing images, conducting audit interviews, and finally, using the results to fix any perceptual gaps the audit might have uncovered.

Case Study: Farrington State College Audits its Visual Identity

Farrington State College was founded in the mid-1800s as a teachers' college for women in eastern Massachusetts. During the early 1900s, the college began to admit men and offer varied majors. By the late 1900s, the college was one of a number of states colleges in the Massachusetts system, many of which offered similar courses and equivalent educations.

By 2005, Farrington State had begun to differentiate itself from the other state colleges by investing in professional programs and an increased number of dormitories. The college had also made a concerted effort to improve its standing in national rankings. Over the previous 10 years, Farrington State had moved from number 47 in its category to number 36. The goal of the college president, Warren Nicholas, was to move into the top 20 by the year 2020. The "20 by 2020" initiative had gained a lot of momentum at the college, due mostly to Nicholas's enthusiasm and commitment.

Nicholas was aware of the resources it would take to reach his goal, and he believed significant resources needed to be focused on drawing attention to the college. While the school was well known in its surrounding region, it had little to no national reputation. Nicholas felt that a marketing effort focused on bringing national attention to the school was integral to fulfilling the college's vision, so he hired Lisa Swanson to spearhead all marketing efforts.

Swanson was new to Farrington State, but she had more than ten years' experience conducting marketing programs for large state universities with national reputations. There were differences between those universities and Farrington State, most notably the absence of an athletic program, but Swanson felt Farrington had a number of unique academic programs to exploit. Swanson also assumed that the college had ignored its visual identity for decades, since what she found was outdated and very inconsistent. Internal documents used a logo that Swanson was able to trace back to the 1980s, but alumni publications used a more modern logo that seemed to more accurately reflect the college today.

A more basic issue was the college's Web site: the URL was www. farrsc.edu, rather than the more obvious www.fsc.edu. Swanson realized that a small private college in a neighboring state, Farmington College, had claimed the fsc.edu address, but she thought there must be a more fitting URL for Farrington State.

To ensure that she was seeing all versions of the visual identity the college was using, Swanson planned a visual identity audit. One of her first official acts at the college involved developing a cross-functional team of communications employees from each of the college's departments, as well as the heads of the alumni, development, and student affairs offices.

When Swanson convened the audit team's first meeting, she began to explain the reason for the visual identity audit. Almost immediately, the heads of the alumni and development offices pushed back against Swanson about their use of the college's visual identity. They made it clear to Swanson that they did not want to change what they were doing. Conversely, the heads of the remaining departments agreed with Swanson that the college seemed to be inconsistent in its use of several elements of its identity, including the colors used in marketing materials.

Although some of them disagreed with the need for the audit, all of the department heads agreed to complete two tasks before the next meeting: each would collect as many internal and external touchpoints as possible, and each would provide a list of internal and external contacts who might agree to be interviewed as part of the audit.

At the next meeting three weeks later, the audit team laid out all of the touchpoints on a large conference table. Even the alumni and development office heads admitted that the college had a problem: there was no consistency, even among internal documents, and each of the departments' materials reflected various evolutions of the logo from the 1980s. In addition, there was no true consistency in the colors used in the materials. The official college colors were maroon and gold, but materials were produced using various shades of red.

Toward of the end of the discussion on the inconsistency of the touchpoints, the team decided to go forward with the interviews. Each department head was now on board with the visual identity audit, so each agreed to have five internal and five external interviews to be completed by the next meeting.

With the interviews complete, at the next meeting each of the department heads spoke about their results. Because of time constraints, some of the departments were not able to complete all of their interviews, but the results were still pretty clear: internal audiences remained very loyal to the college, but they were not quite sure how the college wanted to present itself to the public. Because there was no consistency with its visual presentation, employees felt the college had no readily identifiable "look." Interviews with external publics showed similar, yet more extreme, results. External audiences could not clearly identify the school's signature colors, and some of these same audiences joked that the college had a severe identity crisis.

Case Discussion Questions

1. It is obvious that Farrington State College needs a new URL for its Web site. What should the new URL be? From a communica-

tions perspective, how should the transition to a new URL be managed?

2. If you were Lisa Swanson, what would you do as a next step in the visual identity audit process?

3. Given the inconsistencies in Farrington State's visual identity, should Swanson immediately change the visual identity of the college? If yes, how should she proceed?

Bibliography

Napoles, V. 1988. *Corporate Identity Design.* New York: John Wiley & Sons, Inc.

Olins, W., and E. Selame. 1993. *The Corporate Identity Audit: A Set of Objective Measurement Tools for Your Company's Image and Reputation.* Zurich, Switzerland: Strategic Direction Publishers.

Quelch, J.A. 1998. *Pepsi Blue.* Boston, MA: Harvard Business School Publishing.

Schmitt, B., and A. Simonson. 1997. *Marketing Aesthetics: The Strategic Management of Brands, Identity, and Image.* New York: The Free Press.

"Why Federal Express Became FedEx." n.d. *@issue.* Available at www.cdf.org/issue_journal/why_federal_express_became_fedex.html. Accessed November 18, 2008.

6

Beyond the Law

Protecting Visual Identity from the Inside Out

Imagine a festive child's birthday party. There are the requisite cake, balloons, ice cream, and costumed character—and plenty of happy children. If you look a little closer, however, this otherwise happy occasion could be marred by a potentially illegal act: an unlicensed costumed character—anyone from Thomas the Tank Engine to Elmo to the Incredible Hulk—interacting with the guests at the party.

The costumed character is illegal if it was sold (or rented for a fee) by an organization that did not have the right (a license) to provide the character. While it may seem draconian, the company that owns the trademarked character might just insist that the organization stop selling or renting these costumes:

> Trademark holders say they are trying to protect the integrity of their brands; they don't want Dora to show up at a party with a cigarette dangling from her mouth. Attorneys note that if they do not actively police their trademarks in one realm, a court might later rule that they have forfeited their rights to enforce it in others. (Rosman 2008, p. A1)

Protective Tactics

The focus of this chapter is not the actual trademark infringement (which is discussed in more detail in Chapter 7), but *how* the organizations that own trademarks might become aware of potential infringement. The most vigilant organizations employ a number of proactive measures to protect their visual identity assets. Several of these efforts are discussed in more detail below.

Cease-and-Desist Orders

A cease-and-desist order (also called a C&D letter) is defined as an order that "may be issued upon a showing, to a degree of certainty or probability, that the conduct is unlawful or likely to be found unlawful" (Gifis 1998). These orders are typically issued via a letter to the offending party (in the above scenario, the offender is the provider of the costume). The letter simply states that the offender should stop the offending behavior or risk being taken to court.

> Possibly the greatest advantage of an enforcement program based on sending cease and desist letters is that it can be a relatively low-cost way to resolve many, if not most, trademark infringement matters. In clear-cut cases, the infringers often recognize that it is in their best interest to stop the offending activity and cooperate with the trademark owner to resolve the matter amicably. When infringement is a closer question, a C&D may be the first step toward negotiating bilateral concessions that keep the dispute out of court. (Wilcox 2006)

Employee Involvement in Identity Protection

In addition to invoking the law, when needed, the best way to protect the investment in an organization's visual identity is to build support for it from the inside out. Employees who truly embrace a brand—"brand champions" and "brand ambassadors"—can typically be counted on to protect the organization's visual identity. There are several ways to get employees involved in the organization's protective efforts, several of which are discussed below.

Employee Training

Protecting a visual identity from infringement can be a time-consuming and costly process. By educating employees about the importance of the identity, however, and by training them in various ways to protect it, the process can become a much-simplified and much less expensive one.

Education on organizational visual identity should focus on the importance of using it consistently day to day. Even minor inconsistencies over a long period of time can harm the organization's brand equity, which could result in a diminished brand image.

The question of who within the organization should be trained is best left to the discretion of the organization, depending on its resources, but it would be beneficial to provide at least some training to all employees. This training can come in the form of something as simple as a lunch-hour seminar or something more comprehensive, such as a full-day or two-day workshop. Undoubtedly, educating individual employees across all levels will only bolster the company's overall protective efforts.

What to include in this training is another important consideration. Employees should first be educated on the basics of what the organization's visual identity is, including its function and its value to the organization. In addition, employees should understand that any misuse or infringement of the organization's visual identity could harm the organization's image. Finally, employees should gain a clear understanding of what misuse or infringement of the organization's identity actually looks like—provide examples, whether real or hypothetical, that would illustrate infringement clearly. Another effective way to show infringement is through case studies of *other* organizations that have successfully overcome infringement issues. Each of these case studies or examples should contain clear lessons to be learned.

Schedule an All-Employee Meeting

Conventional wisdom among visual identity researchers states that an organization's visual identity should be managed at the highest levels of the organization (Aaker and Joachimsthaler 2000). In a for-profit firm, the highest level would be the CEO's office, but in a smaller organization (such as a school or a local nonprofit), the highest level might refer to a principal or director. Regardless of the organization's size, employees should realize that visual identity is a concept so important to the organization's livelihood that it is managed by the person responsible for the overall livelihood of the organization.

When the CEO or principal or director of an organization calls a meeting of all employees to discuss the organization's visual identity, employees receive a very strong signal about the importance of visual identity. For this reason, calling a meeting of all employees is a very good way to draw instant attention to the issue, and using the meeting to educate employees lets them know that visual identity is a serious component of the organization's success.

The organization's leader is the natural choice for leading this meeting, since he/she is best suited to articulating the vision of the organization, and explaining how the visual identity fits into the organization's strategy for achieving that vision. Olins and Selame write:

The . . . vision on which the identity is based must be explained clearly and simply. The place of the vision as part of the [organization's] philosophy must be demonstrated. The commitment of management to drive home the vision through communication and behavior as well as through the new visual program must be emphasized. (1993, p. 55)

This meeting with the organization's leadership should not take the place of the aforementioned employee training session, but it does provide a nice lead-in to the training workshops and seminars, as well as an opportunity for the organization's leader to discuss the importance of organizational visual identity.

Finally, as a thank-you to employees for coming to the meeting, consider ordering t-shirts, mugs, or mouse pads in the appropriate color palette with the organization's logo or tagline. This will let them know they are an integral part of the organization's visual identity. They will also provide a consistent level of internal exposure to the visual identity.

Provide a Picture

Visual identity lends itself to pictures, and stimulating the senses is often one of the most effective ways to teach. For this reason, if the organization's budget and time permit, consider producing a visual metaphor—a video, film, or digital montage—to preview at the employee meeting and in training sessions.

This is not an original idea: To win a major automotive advertising account, Boston-based Arnold Communications produced a "brand essence" video to reflect how the agency viewed the automotive brand, but the video also served as a way to energize the client company as it embarked on its advertising campaign. The video was a montage of photos (of employees in the workplace, from movies, TV, and even magazines) set to music that captured the meaning of the identity and the culture it represented. This was a way to give the visual identity and the brand a personality, so it was effective as a visual point of reference.

If the plan is to produce a visual metaphor like this one, it is important to carefully choose only those visuals that are truly representative of the organization's attributes, as employees may begin to "model" the visual identity based on an image they saw in the video. This video is also a good tool for future employee orientation sessions. When it is presented in combination with the visual identity booklet produced for the all-employee meeting (a style guide or "brand book," which will be discussed in greater detail below), new employees get an energetic introduction to the organization's visual identity and culture.

Issue Style Guides

The U.S. Army is a government organization with nearly 500,000 soldiers stationed in the United States and abroad. Each of these soldiers is responsible for wearing his or her uniforms correctly on a daily basis and to special events. Failure to adhere to the rules might be considered a punishable infraction. But with half a million soldiers, each with several uniforms, and each living in different countries and time zones, how do individual soldiers know how to wear each individual insignia appropriately on the correct uniform? In addition to experience, and perhaps sneaking a peak at a fellow soldier, the answer lies in the army's 300-plus page online manual: "Wear and Appearance of Army Uniforms and Insignia" (2005). For example, on page 191, section 28–6, the manual clarifies how to wear the captain's grade insignia:

> The non-subdued grade insignia is two silver-colored bars, each 3/8 inch in width and 1 inch in length, with a smooth surface. The bars are placed 1/4 inch apart and are worn lengthwise on collars, parallel to the shoulder seam on shoulder loops.

Because this type of specificity is crucial to ensuring that army personnel are all wearing their uniforms appropriately, which is integral to projecting the army's visual identity, the army understands the need for a central reference for soldiers and other army personnel. Organizations of all sizes and types also require a kind of reference manual for the proper use of their visual identities. These references go by several names but are generally known as "style guides" or "visual identity manuals." Regardless of the name, the intent is the same: to ensure that everyone responsible for projecting the visual identity has a reference point for using it properly in every conceivable medium.

Because style guides provide very detailed guidelines and offer specific "rules" on using each of the individual elements of the visual identity in advertising, on signage and architecture, and in virtually every other promotional activity, they are typically distributed to only to those employees who work with the visual identity on a daily basis, such as marketing employees and advertising agencies. There is nothing to stop an organization from distributing to all employees, however, to ensure consistency throughout the organization (even on internal documents).

Coca-Cola, one of the world's most recognizable organizations, has a rich history of protecting its visual identity. In a memo running more than two-and-a-half pages, Coca-Cola's counsel outlined a set of rules for the proper use of the Coca-Cola trademark. The first rule stated that the Coca-Cola name was never to be split on two lines of text. Rule 24 dictated that Coca-Cola should never be referred to as "it" (Allen 1994, p. 235). In retrospect, Rule 24 appears especially anachronistic. In 1982, Coca-Cola's "Coke is it!" tagline was introduced.

Monitor the Press

Media attention can be a very cost-efficient way to generate interest in an organization, as well as providing an opportunity to educate both the press and the public on the proper use of the visual identity. For this reason, organizations need to be vigilant about monitoring any newspaper or magazine articles, or any radio or television broadcasts, that mention the organization.

Police the Web

The World Wide Web provides exciting opportunities for organizations of all sizes to present themselves to a global audience, but the Web also presents the potential for rampant infringement of visual identities. Just as organizations need to monitor the press, another way to catch cases of infringement before they occur is to regularly patrol or "police" the Web for unauthorized use of the organization's visual identity. Returning to the example used above regarding the unauthorized characters at birthday parties, the companies that own many of today's most well-known characters also police the Web. General counsel for Marvel, which owns Spider-Man, Captain America, and The Incredible Hulk, believes a company that is built on intellectual property must police the use of its assets. "We don't want to interfere with or ruin the fun of birthday parties. . . . But we do search the Internet all the time for commercial use of our characters" (Rosman 2008, p. A1).

HIT Entertainment, which has a portfolio of characters including

Barney, Bob the Builder, and Thomas the Tank Engine, says the company tries to actively police the world of birthday parties by regularly monitoring birthday-party planning Web sites and parenting blogs (Rosman 2008, p. A1).

Organizations also have the law on their side with respect to policing the Web. In 1997, a federal court ruled in favor of Playboy Enterprises when its name was being embedded in HTML code used by search engines to return search results (Lastowka 2000). The court stated that it was an infringement of Playboy Enterprises trademarks to use them "in buried code or metatags on their home page or Web pages, or in connection with the retrieval of data or information or on other goods or services, or in connection with the advertising or promotion of their goods, services or web sites" (*Playboy Enterprises, Inc., v. Calvin Designer Label* 1997).

Even with its tremendous resources and its typical vigilance against infringers, Coca-Cola has also had to combat infringement of its visual identity online. Employees whose job it was to patrol the Web for potential infringement found a pornographic Web site employing the famous Coca-Cola contour bottle (Bulik 2000).

There are companies that offer this type of service for a fee, but organizations can achieve the same objective by conducting systematic searches on commercial search engines. If a company does not have the human resources to devote to this task on a full-time basis, a coordinated volunteer effort may work if employees are offered an appropriate incentive.

Share What Other Organizations Do

One way of demonstrating to employees the value of the organization's visual identity is to share stories of the extreme ways some other organizations protect theirs. In Chapter 7, there is a discussion of how Coca-Cola employed a Trade Research Department whose job it was to travel around the country, order Coca-Cola in a restaurant, and then send a sample back to Atlanta to ensure that said drink was actually Coca-Cola. Those trying to pass off Pepsi and other cola products as Coke were sued by the company for contributory trademark infringement (Koten 1978). While many organizations may not have the resources afforded a multinational company, this story does serve to show how seriously Coca-Cola protects its visual identity.

Instill Pride in the Identity

There might be no better way to inspire employees to protect the organization's visual identity than to get them directly involved in promoting it. For example, many organizations will sponsor naming contests among employees if an organizational name change is planned. While this may not be the most strategically sound decision for every organization, smaller ones would certainly find it the most cost efficient (as opposed to hiring a professional naming agency or visual identity firm).

There are also myriad other ways to directly involve employees in promoting the visual identity. If your organization plans an advertising campaign or is producing a glossy annual report, consider using employees or their families as the models or talent. In addition to instilling pride in individual employees, the use of actual employees in promotional materials sends a message about the pride the organization has in its employees. For example, Wal-Mart features its employees and their families in sale fliers. In the financial services industry, Deloitte and Touche featured its employees in a corporate advertising campaign as a way of demonstrating that the employees are the company's most valuable assets. More recently, Johnson & Johnson developed a Tylenol advertising campaign that featured employees who actually make the product exclaiming that they make the product "with love" (Crain 2007).

Provide a Go-To Employee

Regardless of where employees work within an organization, everyone should be aware of whom to contact with questions related to the organization's visual identity. If your organization does not already have a "logo guru," consider assigning one or two. This responsibility will differ depending on the size and scope of the organization, but one way to ensure consistency is to assign a marketing manager the responsibility for answering questions related to external communications, including public relations and advertising; the employee communications liaison should be the contact person for questions related to internal use of the visual identity. Regardless of how the organization assigns responsibility, those responsible should be so familiar with the proper use of the visual identity that they know if it is being reproduced as set forth in the style guide: for example, white space around the logo meets specifications, the typeface is the right size, and the color is being reproduced in the appropriate shade.

Provide Templates

On a day-to-day basis, organizations of all sizes send faxes and produce memos, reports, and slide presentations for a variety of purposes. Whether those materials are for internal or external consumption, each presents an opportunity to reflect and reinforce the organization's visual identity.

The most efficient way to ensure consistent use of the visual identity by every member of the organization is for the employee communications department to prepare and distribute templates for departmental and organization-wide memos, fax cover sheets, report covers, and slide presentations, in addition to any other communication vehicles the organization might use on a regular basis. These templates will provide employees with a no-hassle approach to communication while ensuring consistent use of the visual identity.

Model the Appropriate Language

The legal protection afforded an organization's visual identity by trademark law is the most concrete way to protect the various elements of the visual identity, but that does not preclude the need to educate employees on their contribution to protecting the organization's trademarks. One of the most important ways to educate employees on how to discuss the organization's trademarks is to model appropriate language use.

An easy rule of thumb for remembering how to refer to trademarks is to remember that trademarks should always be used as adjectives (e.g., Kleenex tissues)—never as nouns—when referred to in conversations and in the text of any communication, whether internal or external. This prevents the trademark from "genericide," the fate that befell the previously trademarked "aspirin" and "escalator" when they were used to describe the product category rather than a specific brand.

Summary

Every organization has a visual identity, so every organization is at risk for infringement of its visual identity. One way to minimize the risk of such infringement is to sufficiently monitor the public's use of the visual identity. By explicitly engaging the legal protections afforded by intellectual property law, including sending cease-and-desist orders, an organization can vigilantly protect its visual identity. By involving employees, however, the organization can protect its investment in its visual identity while simultaneously educating employees on its importance to the organization. The ways to involve and train employees should start with scheduling an all-employee meeting so that employees can hear about the visual identity's value from an organizational leader. Other ways to educate employees and inspire them to monitor the visual identity's use include issuing style guides and training employees to monitor the press and police the Web. Sharing whatever tactics other organizations employ to protect their visual identities is a good way to draw parallels between organizations, as well as to introduce new techniques for pro-tection. Finally, to ensure that employees understand that everyone in the organization will be expected to monitor the proper use of the visual identity, organizations should provide templates, model the appropriate language, and provide the contact information for one employee whose purview it is to answer questions related to visual identity.

Case Study: Protecting the "Lovin' Stuff" Visual Identity from Itself

With her two young children in school full-time, Hannah Kelley found herself missing her former career as a marketing manager. She thought the remedy for this might be a part-time job, so she began searching and quickly came upon the perfect opportunity: a few hours a week helping out the creator of a new line of children's stuffed toys.

During the interview, Kelley found that she really liked Nina Corcoran, the brains behind the "Lovin' Stuff" brand of children's toys and the company's founder. Corcoran had a vision for the company that Kelley admired: Corcoran believed her toys could help children develop both emotionally and intellectually, and she wanted to do everything she could to help the company grow quickly yet strategically.

Kelley had been working for Corcoran for several weeks when it became clear to both women that Kelley was far too qualified to simply answer phones and file invoices. It also became clear that Corcoran was too busy working on developing the actual "Lovin' Stuff" product to provide Kelley with much guidance on new projects.

While filing the last of the invoices one day, and putting the accom-panying checks into the nightly deposit bag, Kelley noticed that many of the checks had several different versions of the company's name on them. She also realized that every time she answered the phone, she did so slightly differently: sometimes saying just the name of the company, and other times saying the name of the company before also telling the caller her name and asking how she might help them.

Later that day, working on a hunch, Kelley decided to ask Corcoran if she could look at all of the press that had been generated about "Lovin' Stuff." Corcoran looked at Kelley blankly and stated that she'd read some articles about her company but had never bothered to clip any of it. She was always too busy and figured she could do it later.

The next week at work, Kelley and Corcoran carved out some time to meet to discuss Kelley's ideas on how she might use her time to help Corcoran protect her investment in her company by helping her protect her visual identity. Corcoran did not immediately understand what Kelley meant, but came to the conclusion that Kelley sounded like she knew what she was doing.

Over the next several days, Kelley began to comb through Corcoran's official business documents—everything from her business plan, which successfully attracted investors, to the documents relating to incorpora-tion and trademarks. What she found were a number of different names used for the company and product, each a slight variation on the name used in the original business plan. The variations were slight, and mostly grammatical—from "Loving Stuff" to "Love and Stuff." It was clear that Corcoran had not paid a lot of attention to visual identity issues, yet she'd been very successful building her company and selling her product.

Kelley found Corcoran's own misuse of her company and product names alarming, since Corcoran could eventually run into trouble if her business grew so far and so fast that the public would be confused about what the company and product names actually were. Luckily, Corcoran gave Kelley free reign to pursue integrity of the company's visual identity.

Shortly after her conversation with Corcoran, Kelley began to make a list of the company and product names that Corcoran had used in her own materials. After doing this internal search, Kelley moved onto the external environment: she started with a simple Web search on all three names she uncovered during her internal search. The results were surpris-ing: Kelley found many press articles touting the company and product, but she also found several Web sites panning the product, and even a few infringing the company's official trademark. Kelley wrote up a report for Corcoran and started to think about her next steps.

After a week spent researching the use and misuse of the "Lovin' Stuff" visual identity, Kelley was looking forward to a quiet Saturday. She headed out the door with her children toward a neighborhood birthday party. When she arrived, she noticed the cake. A local bakery had iced a large "Lovin' Stuff" product logo on the cake's top tier.

Case Discussion Questions

1. Discuss the implications of Nina Corcoran's vague understanding of her company and product's visual identity.
2. If you were in Hannah Kelley's position, would you have approached the visual identity issues the same way? If not, what would be your approach?
3. What should Hannah Kelley do with all of the information she's collected from the press and the Web?
4. Does Hannah Kelley's job end when she leaves the office? Should she do or say anything about the child's birthday cake?

Bibliography

Aaker, D.A., and E. Joachimsthaler. 2000. *Brand Leadership*. New York: Free Press.

Allen, F. 1994. *Secret Formula: How Brilliant Marketing and Relentless Salesmanship Made Coca-Cola the Best-Known Product in the World*. New York: HarperCollins.

Bulik, B.S. 2000. "The Brand Police." *Business 2.0.*, November 28, pp. 144–55.

Crain, R. 2007. "Hold the Love, J&J—We'd Rather Have Honesty in Our Tylenol Ads." *Advertising Age*, November 26, p. 15.

Gifis, S.H. 1998. *Dictionary of Legal Terms*. 3rd ed. Hauppauge, NY: Barron's Educational Series.

Koten, J. 1978. "Mixing with Coke over Trademarks Always a Fizzle; Coca-Cola Adds a Little Life in Court to Those Failing to Serve the Real Thing." *Wall Street Journal*, March 9, p. 1.

Lastowka, F.G. 2000. "Search Engines, HTML, and Trademarks: What's the Meta For?" *Virginia Law Review* 86 (May): 835–884.

Olins, W., and E. Selame. 1993. *The Corporate Identity Audit: A Set of Objective Measurement Tools for Your Company's Image and Reputation*. Zurich, Switzerland: Strategic Direction Publishers.

Playboy Enterprises, Inc., v. Calvin Designer Label. 1997. No. C-97-3204 CAL. United States District Court, N.D. California. September 8.

Rosman, K. 2008. "Why Dora the Explorer Can't Come To Your Kid's Birthday Party. The Issue Is Trademark Infringement; Invite SpongeBob, Get SquishyGuy." *Wall Street Journal*, July 22, p. A1.

"Wear and Appearance of Army Uniforms and Insignia." 2005. United States Army. Available at www.fas.org/irp/doddir/army/ar670-1.pdf. Accessed April 21, 2009.

Wilcox, D.A. 2006. "Resist Cease and Desist: A Lighter Approach May Work Better with Trademarks." *Business Law Today* (May/June), p. 27.

7

Trademark Law

*[Trademarks] are the closest a giant corporation can come to
anthropomorphizing itself, to presenting a face, a personality;
they are a way of bringing into being something that is
enormously far-reaching, complicated, many-faceted,
and in many cases not even tangible.*
—Barbara Baer Capitman (1976)

For centuries, business owners have used marks to denote the ownership of goods. Cattle owners in Egypt branded their cattle as a way of
tracking their herds, and after the cattle were sold, the brand served as
the mark of the seller (Ruston 1955). Throughout history, markings have
been used to denote source and identity, from the Hindus' use of marks
in trade between India and Asia Minor from 1300 to 1200 B.C.E. to the
coats of arms used during medieval times (Diamond 1983).

More modern use of "maker's marks" developed in pre-revolutionary
England as a way of identifying the source and quality of silversmiths'
work (Rainwater 1966). In post-Revolutionary America, colonial artisans
adopted the English silversmiths' tradition and used "pseudo hallmarks"
to indicate their silver's origin.

At the end of the nineteenth century, the Industrial Revolution gave
rise to the proliferation of trademarks used to denote the origin and
quality of goods. Between 1860 and 1920, the United States underwent
a major transition—from a marketplace filled with bulk goods to a
marketplace of goods bearing the identifiable marks, the trademarks,
of their manufacturers. With increased competition to sell seemingly
equivalent products, manufacturers began advertising their brand names
and trademarks. Manufacturers also began to use product packaging as a
medium for extolling a product's virtues. In 1887, Log Cabin maple syrup
appeared on grocery-store shelves in cabin-shaped packages. Makers
of Log Cabin syrup "soon found that customers willingly paid extra for

the novelty, as well as for the convenience and product assurance they gained" (Sivulka 1998, p. 52).

While there is no definitive origin of the field of visual identity, it is generally believed to be linked with the evolution of trademark law. Many believe that the visual identity industry was officially developed during the 1960s when Walter Margulies of Lippincott and Margulies coined the phrase "corporate identity" (DeNeve 1989; Margulies 1977).

In 1988, the Lanham Act underwent its first major revision since it was enacted in 1947 (Kitch and Perlman 1998). The resulting Trademark Law Revision Act provided an intent-to-use provision that allows firms to claim trademark rights in advance of registration based on a good-faith intent to use the trademark in commerce. This change in the law provides more flexibility for organizations planning and developing the elements of their visual identities.

Marketers and organizational leaders do not need to be lawyers. But keeping in mind that a trademark provides the organization with ownership of the visual identity, there are several basics about trademark law that organizations should be aware of in order to keep their organizations and visual identities protected.

What Is a Trademark?

In 1928, Judge Learned Hand articulated the idea of a trademark as an integral part of an organization's reputation. He wrote in an opinion for the Second Circuit Court of Appeals:

> [The merchant's] mark is his authentic seal; by it he vouches for the goods which bear it; it carries his name for good or ill. If another uses it, he borrows the owner's reputation, whose quality no longer lies within his own control. This is an injury, even though the borrower does not tarnish it, or divert sales by its use; for a reputation, like a face, is the symbol of its possessor and creator, and another can use it only as a mark. (*Yale Electric Corporation v. Robertson, Commissioner of Patents* 1928)

Judge Hand was clearly ahead of his time, since it took nearly twenty more years for the federal government to bring structure to trademark law. In July 1947, the Lanham Act began to provide federal protection to trademarks, which are defined in the act as

> Any word, name, symbol, or device, or any combination thereof: 1) used by a person, or 2) which a person has a bona fide intention to use in commerce

and applies to register on the principal register established by this Act, to identify and distinguish his or her goods, including a unique product, from those manufactured or sold by others and to indicate the source of the goods, even if that source is unknown. (U.S. Congress, 15 USC § 1127)

There are a variety of types of trademarks, so the key to protecting an organization's trademarks is to know how—and if—the law recognizes the mark.

Trade Name

A trade name—simply the name the organization uses in trade—identifies the organization but not its products or services, and therefore is only eligible for registration and protection by trademark law when the trade name is also used as a trademark (McCarthy 1999). For example, the Coca-Cola Company is the soda firm's trade name, but "Coca-Cola" is a registered trademark since it also serves as the name of the firm's flagship brand of soda.

Certification Mark

A certification mark signifies compliance with a set of predefined standards. This type of mark is used with permission by someone other than its owner to certify the characteristics of a seller's goods or services. The UL symbol, conferred by Underwriters Laboratory, Inc., is a well-known certification mark that lets consumers know a product has passed a rigorous safety test and is in compliance with the UL's safety standards.

Collective Mark

A collective mark is intended to be used in commerce by the members of a group or organization. One of the most famous collective marks, "Realtor," belongs to the National Association of Realtors and indicates a real estate agent's membership in the association.

Trademark Classification

The monopoly manifest in trademark ownership prevents others from using similar trademarks as identifiers of their products (McClure 1979), but the strength of trademark protection varies in proportion to the strength of the trademark itself. The United States Patent and Trademark Office (USPTO) uses a classification system to determine if a trademark is worthy of registration, and the courts consult these classifications to determine if a trademark deserves protection under the Lanham Act when a case of infringement is brought. However, these classifications are less than definitive. Kitch and Perlman (1998) warn, "These categories, like the tones in a spectrum, tend to blur at the edges and merge together. The labels are more advisory than definitional, more like guidelines than pigeonholes" (p. 185). The generally accepted trademark classification system delineates four types of trademarks: generic, descriptive, suggestive, and arbitrary or fanciful.

Generic

A generic term is the term generally used for the product category itself; it refers to a broad range of products rather than to a specific brand name. This type of trademark is never afforded protection under the Lanham Act. Moreover, a protected mark that later becomes generic is subject to cancellation of its registration.

Descriptive

A descriptive term identifies a specific characteristic of a product, such as its color, function, or ingredients, and may be afforded trademark protection under the Lanham Act only with a showing that the descriptive term has a secondary meaning associated with the organization's visual identity. The generally accepted legal definition of secondary meaning dates back to 1912. According to Judge Denison in *G. and C. Merriam Co. v. Saalfield* (1912), secondary meaning is defined as follows:

> It contemplates that a word or phrase originally . . . ha[s] been used so long and so exclusively by one producer with reference to his article that, in that trade and to that branch of the purchasing public, the word or phrase had come to mean that the article was his product; in other words, had come to be, to them, his trade-mark. So it was said that the word had come to have a secondary meaning.

Suggestive

A suggestive term, as the name implies, suggests a characteristic of a product and is afforded trademark protection under the Lanham Act without a showing of secondary meaning associated with the product or organization. As Judge Learned Hand observed in *Canal Co. v. Clark*, "The validity of the mark ends where suggestion ends and description begins" (McClure 1979).

Arbitrary or Fanciful

The strongest types of trademarks in this classification scheme are arbitrary or fanciful terms—such as Ivory soap and Kodak cameras, respectively—that in no way describe the characteristics of the product to which they apply. These terms are eligible for protection under the Lanham Act without a showing of secondary meaning associated with the organization (Kitch and Perlman 1998).

Beyond the Singular Trademark

In addition to the standard trademark classifications, the law also recognizes elements of a visual identity that are a bit more difficult to classify. For example, the "gestalt" of an organization, or the unified look of it, such as through its interior design (its "trade dress"), may be protected under the Lanham Act. Organizations might also use a sensory branding approach and employ color, sounds, or scents as part of their visual identities.

"Trade Dress"

Trade dress is typically regarded as the overall appearance of a product, and it may include package design or even interior design. In 1992, the Supreme Court held that secondary meaning is not required to prevail on an infringement claim when the trade dress is inherently distinctive (*Two Pesos v. Taco Cabana*, 505 U.S. 763, 1992).

In the case of Taco Cabana, the trade dress was the unique interior design of a Mexican theme restaurant. Taco Cabana claimed that Two Pesos, another Mexican theme restaurant, copied its distinctive interior design. Although the two restaurants were not originally competitors due to geography, eventually they began operating in several of the same Texas cities using similar decor. In 1987, Taco Cabana sued Two Pesos for trade dress infringement. The Supreme Court eventually allowed Taco Cabana to prevail in its infringement claim.

Sound as a Trademark

By the 1970s—about the same time visual identity consultancies (such as Lippincott and Margulies) were developing—the scope of trademark law broadened to encompass auditory trademarks. In 1971, the NBC network was granted service-mark registration of its "three chimes." The description of the mark maintained by the USPTO reads:

> The mark comprises a sequence of chime-like musical notes which are in the key of C and sound the notes G, E, C, the "G" being the one just below middle C, the "E" the one just above middle C, and the "C" being middle C, thereby to identify applicant's broadcasting service. (http://tarr.uspto.gov/)

For years, Harley-Davidson motorcycle company had an application pending with the U.S. Patent and Trademark Office to trademark the sound of its "common crankpin V-Twin engine" (Sapherstein 1998). Harley-Davidson believed its engine's roar distinguished it from other motorcycles, and the company wanted to make sure that no other company was able to copy this unique sound (Sapherstein 1998). While Harley-Davidson eventually withdrew its application in 2000, the government has recognized that sounds make up an important part of an organization's visual identity.

Although there are very few actual sound trademarks registered with the USPTO today, there are many organizations that recognize that specific sounds can be an effective part of their visual identities. The most easily recognizable of these might be the sounds emanating from retail stories. All Starbucks stores around the country project the same type and volume of music; Abercrombie & Fitch stores do this as well. Even if you cannot identify the exact musical composition, the sound itself has become closely associated with the store.

Color as a Trademark

Several well-known firms have registered their corporate colors as trademarks. In the mid-1990s, when Pepsi-Cola decided to differentiate itself from Coca-Cola by using one predominant color for its marketing communications, it registered its "Pepsi Blue" color (Johnson 1998). In 1916, UPS began using the color brown on some of its vehicles; by

1929 the firm's entire fleet was painted brown. The firm trademarked its color—referred to as "UPS Brown"—and in early 2002 began the largest advertising campaign in the company's ninety-five-year history in order to promote the firm's longtime association with the color brown (Elliott 2002).

Scent as a Trademark

The law has recognized that some products can be identified simply by their scent. In order to be eligible for protection, the scent must not have a functional value, such as a perfume or scented household cleaner. Instead, the scent is so closely aligned with the product or organization that it actually serves to identify the organization (Brookman 1999).

The first trademark scent was registered in 1991 and identified the maker of embroidery thread. The trademark description reads: "the mark is a high impact, fresh, floral fragrance reminiscent of plumeria blossoms" (http://tarr.uspto.gov/).

Trademark Registration Process

Organizations must take steps to protect their trademarks. The most basic way to protect a trademark is to use the proper trademark symbol alongside it. This serves as notice to the public that the trademark is owned by the organization (see further discussion below).

The process for registering—and ultimately protecting—a trademark should begin with the development of the visual identity. The first step in the trademark process is to ensure that the chosen trademark fits into the proper classification category. Once the organization has ensured that the elements are generally protectable, the organization should search the online USPTO database of existing trademarks to ensure that the specific trademark can be protected. Once these preliminary steps are completed, the process of filing the paperwork may begin.

While a trademark lawyer is not required to register for a trademark on behalf of an organization, hiring an attorney is recommended because there are many steps in the process and many nuances in the law that can make the process more difficult for those not accustomed to it.

Table 7.1

The Meaning of Trademark Symbols

Symbol	Symbol Meaning
™	This serves as notice of a claim of rights in a trademark; it provides some protection from infringement, but should only be used until the trademark has achieved registered status. This symbol may be used immediately upon creation of the trademark.
SM	This serves as notice of a claim of rights in a service mark, which identifies a service rather than product. Its denotation is the same as the TM symbol.
®	This denotes federally registered trademark status. It provides exclusive rights to a trademark, and denotes "ownership" and absolute protection from trademark infringement.

Trademark Symbols

The Lanham Act recognizes that there are different levels of trademark protection, from simply claiming rights in a mark, to full-fledged registration of a trademark. These levels are recognized through a series of symbols that help to communicate to the public about the trademark's status. These specific symbols are detailed and summarized in Table 7.1.

Each of these symbols has a specific meaning, and each must always be used in the prescribed ways. For example, an organization needs to be aware that using the ® symbol without actual registered trademark status can result in a charge of deceptive advertising.

An organization that fails to register its trademarks with the USPTO may be gambling with the integrity of its visual identity. Registration brings with it the right to use a trademark symbol (®), which serves as constructive notice to infringers; this constructive notice dictates that an infringer is liable for damages. Conversely, if the organization is employing the ™ symbol because it has not received registered status, there is no constructive notice to infringers until a cease-and-desist letter is sent to serve as official notice. Only after the trademark owner has sent a letter to the defendant is the defendant liable for damages resulting from the infringement.

Violations of Trademark Law

Infringement

Trademark registration provides basic legal protection from infringement, but trademark owners must be able to prove that use of a similar mark, presumably by a competitor, is likely to confuse consumers in the marketplace. In order to determine if a trademark is likely to cause confusion, the court uses a set of eight factors:

1. The strength of the plaintiff's trademark
2. The similarity of the plaintiff's and defendant's trademarks
3. The similarity of the two organizations' trade channels
4. The similarity of the goods offered by the two organizations
5. The sophistication of the market's buyers
6. The degree of care likely to be exercised by the consumers during their purchase
7. The issue of bridging the gap—whether the plaintiff crosses over into areas of business currently served by the defendant
8. The geographic extent of the trade channels served by the plaintiff and defendant (*Polaroid Corporation v. Polarad Electronics Corporation* 1961).

Contributory Trademark Infringement

Organizations are the first line of defense when it comes to trademark protection, but many organizations also have stakeholders or affiliates that also employ the organization's trademarks. One such example is the relationship some organizations have with their vendors. While the organization that owns the trademark may protect the trademark vigilantly, any organization that also employs the trademark might not be as vigilant. One standout example is in the soda industry.

The concept of contributory trademark infringement is clearly illustrated through a legendary Coca-Cola story: Coca-Cola once employed brand stewards whose job included visiting restaurants and ordering a Coca-Cola. If they thought they had been served a substitute brand without being told that the restaurant did not serve Coca-Cola, the stewards would send the specimen back to Atlanta for chemical analysis. Those serving a non-Coca-Cola brand to people who asked for Coke were then sued for contributory trademark infringement (Koten 1978).

The Internet and Trademark Infringement

The Internet, with its uncanny ability to alter the perspective of size, location, and source, presents organizations with both a tremendous opportunity and a serious burden related to trademarks. As a tool for conducting electronic commerce and promoting the organization itself, the Web can expand an organization's reach globally. With global exposure of a visual identity, however, comes an increased risk that an organization's identity will be infringed.

In the early days of e-commerce, "cybersquatters" registered domain names that were registered trademarks of other firms. After the cybersquatter obtained domain name registration, he would offer the domain name to the trademark's rightful owner for a "tidy profit" (Wright and Potenza 1999). This reality brought about the need for legislation to protect trademark owners in cyberspace. The Anti-Cybersquatting Act of 1999 provides civil liability when the trademark owner can prove four elements of the crime:

1. That the defendant registered the domain name
2. That the plaintiff had rights in the trademark at the time the domain name was registered by the defendant
3. That the trademark was a distinctive mark at the time the domain name was registered by the defendant
4. That the defendant registered the domain name in bad faith, with the intention of profiting from extorting the trademark's rightful owner.

There is also a free-speech element to trademark law in the netherworld known as cyberspace. The courts have rooted the right to develop "disparagement" sites (known colloquially as "sucks sites" since they are often named walmartsucks.com or verizonreallysucks.com, for example) in the public's First Amendment right to free speech. This right of free speech intersects with trademark law because the courts have ruled that the public is not likely to think that the firm being disparaged is the sponsor of the site, so the required legal standard of likelihood of confusion, as required under the Lanham Act, is not met.

Ironically, while the courts have condoned disparaging firms in cyberspace, the right to praise firms raises a viable trademark infringement issue. "Fan sites" registered by private individuals as a way to praise brands or firms may be found to infringe trademarks since visitors to the site might be confused into believing the firm being praised is also the source of the Web site. (Kopp and Suter 2000)

Emerging Trademark Issues and the Internet

Because the Internet has proven to be both a revolutionary and evolutionary tool for marketers, there are a number of benefits to using it as a way to promote and reinforce a visual identity. However, there are also a number of emerging issues, as well as those still unknown, that can be harmful to an organization's visual identity.

Serious and emerging issues of trademark protection on the Web concern search engines selling the use of trademarks as paid keyword searches to parties other than the trademark's rightful owner, and their use in unauthorized viral marketing programs. The most effective way to protect a trademark from these and other emerging threats is to patrol the Web on a regular basis (this type of protective effort is discussed in Chapter 6).

Abandonment

According to the Lanham Act, an organization may abandon a trademark in one of two ways: either by an explicit choice to stop using the trademark, or by a failure to properly protect it. An organization may choose to voluntarily abandon a trademark because it has no intent to resume using it, such as when an organization changes one or more elements of its visual identity. Not using a trademark for three consecutive years is evidence of abandonment, which means that the trademark will eventually be available for use by another organization.

In 1993, consumer goods manufacturer Procter & Gamble discontinued manufacturing its White Cloud toilet paper and allowed its registered trademark to lapse. When the trademark was available, a private entrepreneur arranged to sell it to Wal-Mart, which began to distribute diapers under the White Cloud brand (Ellison, Zimmerman, and Forrelle, 2005). This type of trademark abandonment was the result of a conscious decision by Procter & Gamble, but abandonment can also occur as a result of the organization's failure to protect the trademark.

Fueroghne (2000) warns of the dangers of using marketing to position a trademark in a way that might hurt the firm's right to exclusivity of the trademark: "The strength of positioning strategy cannot be questioned. But what is good for marketing may be terrible for protection of a trademark. The advertiser must be careful not to destroy a trademark in the process of building brand awareness" (p. 296).

An organization's explicit or implicit behavior might signify a failure to protect a trademark. Explicit marketing actions—such as not using the appropriate trademark symbols, or using the trademark in advertising copy as a noun rather than an adjective—could cause the trademark to become the generic name for the product category.

Ries and Trout (1986) defend the value of a generic brand name, but this "genericide," or the loss of a trademark through abandonment when the trademark becomes the generic term for a product category, can mean the loss of the trademark. Examples are plentiful: cellophane, linoleum, milk of magnesia, dry ice, aspirin, thermos, and escalator.

Dilution

As early as 1927, even before the Lanham Act granted protection from trademark infringement on a federal level, Schechter (1927) warned that trademarks were being diluted—that is, the power of their message was being "whittled away" by competitors in other markets:

> Trademark pirates are growing more subtle and refined. They proceed circumspectly, by suggestion and approximation, rather than by direct and exact duplication of their victims' wares and marks. The history of important trademark litigation within recent years shows that the use of similar marks on *non*-competing goods is perhaps the *normal* rather than the exceptional case of infringement. (p. 825).

Recognizing that trademark dilution was a practical issue that needed to be addressed for the most well-known trademarks in the United States, Congress passed the Federal Trademark Dilution Act (FTDA) in 1995 to protect "famous" trademarks from dilution by use on noncompeting goods. Although Congress never explicitly defined "famous," the FTDA defines dilution as

> The lessening of the capacity of a famous mark to identify and distinguish goods or services, regardless of the presence or absence of: (1) competition

between the owner of the famous mark and other parties, or (2) likelihood of confusion, mistake, or deception. (U.S. Congress, Federal Trademark Dilution Act, 15 USC § 1127)

Because the law does not explicitly define "famous," the FTDA provides a set of eight factors the court can use as a guideline in determining if a trademark is famous:

1. The distinctiveness of the trademark
2. The duration and extent of the trademark's use
3. The advertising and publicity history of the trademark
4. The geographical extent of the trademark's trading areas
5. The trademark's channels of trade
6. The trademark's degree of recognition in the channels of trade
7. The nature and extent of use of the same or similar trademarks by third parties
8. Whether the trademark was registered (U.S. Congress, Federal Trademark Dilution Act, 15 USC 1125 [c]).

Counterfeiting

Perhaps the most insidious and harmful type of trademark infringement, counterfeiting is the only type of trademark infringement that is criminally—but also civilly—punishable under the law. In the Trademark Counterfeiting Act of 1984, Congress defines a counterfeit trademark as a phony trademark used in connection with trafficked goods or services that is identical to, or indistinguishable from, an actual registered trademark for those goods or services. The counterfeit mark must be likely to cause confusion, mistake, or deception (Goldstone and Toren 1998).

Anecdotally, trademark counterfeiting is believed to cost U.S. industry billions, and it has been deemed "the crime of the 21st century" by the Federal Bureau of Investigation's division on organized crime and drugs (Stipp 1996). According to one counterfeiter, however, selling phony merchandise is sometimes viewed as a public service rather than a crime:

[Counterfeiting's] not hurting anybody. None of my customers think my stuff is real. . . . People can't afford the real stuff. Take Chanel. Their quality is great, but the bags aren't worth the price people pay. They have

---

Figure 7.1
Burberry Trademark Notice

We have used the Burberry Check as a sign of origin since 1924. It is registered as a trade mark throughout the world. Our Burberry name and Equestrian Knight Device are also registered trade marks.

Anyone who uses our name, our Equestrian Knight Device or a check identical with or confusingly similar to our Burberry Check without our permission is infringing our trade marks and will hear from our lawyers.

Source: http://www.burberry.com/Legal.html.
Copyright Burberry, used with permission.

$2,800 bags I'll sell you for $150. . . . We're doing a service by allowing people to have a dream. (p. 140)

While most often associated with luxury fashion products, counterfeiters have also trafficked in pharmaceuticals, infant formula, heart pumps, and other lifesaving products. In addition to potentially endangering human life, trademark counterfeiting affects the entire system of trademarks by affecting the public's perception of the quality of trademarked goods (Goldstone and Toren 1998).

As a federal offense, the burden of proof against trademark counterfeiters is on the government. The law requires proof beyond a reasonable doubt that the defendant intentionally trafficked or attempted to traffic in goods or services knowingly using a counterfeit trademark. The law does not require that sales by the rightful trademark owner be diminished, or that the product with the counterfeit trademark be faulty, or that the counterfeit product be of lesser quality than the one made by the rightful trademark owner (Goldstone and Toren 1998).

Because the incidence of counterfeiting has grown exponentially with advances in technology, organizations have taken it upon themselves to educate the public about the importance of their trademarks. Figure 7.1 contains a trademark statement that appears on the Burberry Web site. Other organizations, as a way to educate the public about trademark counterfeiting, take a consumer-based approach to trademark protection.

Figure 7.2
Kate Spade Trademark Notice

how can i tell if a kate spade bag is authentic?

the craftsmanship of kate spade handbags, as well as the quality of materials used for all products, is unparalleled in comparison to non-authentic merchandise. a label with a country of origin within the bag, as well as a label that is sewn onto the front of the bag, are basic signs of an authentic kate spade handbag. in addition, you can be confident when making your purchase from an authorized kate spade retailer.

the kate spade trademark is a registered trademark throughout the world. use of the kate spade name without permission is considered counterfeiting and warrants legal action. authentic kate spade products are not sold at "purse parties" or at flea markets. they are also not available in new york's chinatown, or santee alley in los angeles. you are also not able to purchase kate spade in kiosks in malls or on auction sites. if a kate spade product is purchased in any of these places, risk of being defrauded is highly likely. the sale and distribution of counterfeit product is a crime under federal and many state laws, and is punishable by imprisonment and fines. the manufacturers of counterfeit products do not pay taxes, do not pay fair wages or benefits to their employees, frequently utilize child labor, and have been known to fund terrorism and other serious crimes with the profits of counterfeiting.

if you would like to submit information on a suspected seller of counterfeit kate spade products, please use our counterfeit reporting document and send it to trademark@liz.com.

thank you for your concern regarding this serious matter.

Source: http://www.katespade.com/helpdesk/index.jsp?display=faq&subdisplay=product. Copyright Kate Spade LLC, used with permission.

The statement in Figure 7.2 appears on fashion designer Kate Spade's Web site.

It is of the utmost importance for organizations to protect their trademarks, but while the law recognizes the organization's right to profit from its investment in a trademark, it also recognizes the right of the public to fairly use the trademark under certain conditions.

Fair Use of Trademarks

If an organization feels that its trademark has been infringed, it should bring legal action against the offending party. However, it is in the organization's best interest to know that plaintiffs might feel as if they have the right to use the trademark in a particular context, thereby mounting a "fair-use defense" to the infringement claim.

The fair-use defense will be examined by the court in light of several factors, including how the trademark is used. For example, is it used prominently to describe the defendant's product or service, or is it used secondarily to other words and features that describe the defendant's product or service?

The second factor the court will look at is whether the defendant is trying to profit from the plaintiff's goodwill by using its trademark. If the defendant is justified in using the trademark to describe his own product, the court would likely find this a fair use of the trademark.

Finally, the court will consider the likelihood that the defendant's use of the plaintiff's trademark is confusing the public about the origin of the product or service. If there is a great likelihood of confusion, the court would likely find that using the trademark was not a fair use.

Summary

For centuries, business owners have been using marks to denote the ownership of goods. Over the past several decades, the American legal system has provided protection for the individual and collective elements of an organization's visual identity. The law is embodied in the Lanham Act, or trademark law, and can provide collective protection for the visual identity, but also individually for logos, colors, and taglines.

Under the Lanham Act, a trademark is defined as "any word, name, symbol, or device" that identifies the source of goods or services. There is a trademark classification system that delineates four types of trademarks—generic, descriptive, suggestive, and arbitrary or fanciful—and is used to determine if a trademark deserves protection. The law also recognizes "trade dress"—the unified look of an organization—and a sensory branding approach that employs sounds, scents, and color is also eligible for protection under the Lanham Act.

Once an organization has a trademark, it is incumbent upon it to protect the mark. The most basic way to protect a trademark is to use the proper trademark symbol alongside it. This serves as notice to the public that the trademark is owned by the organization. An organization that does not vigilantly protect its trademarks may be confronted by one of a number of threats—infringement, abandonment, dilution, or counterfeiting.

If an organization feels that its trademark has been infringed, it should bring legal action against the offending party. However, it is in the organization's best interest to know that plaintiffs might feel as if they have the right to use the trademark in a particular context, thereby mounting a "fair-use defense" to the infringement claim. Under a fair-use defense, the court would consider several factors.

Case Study: Careline, Inc.

Careline, Inc., was founded in 1991 as a service for new mothers who were at home with their infants and needed advice on everything from diapers to colic. Careline built its reputation on being a sort of "phone companion" for women who might be feeling intimidated or unsure of themselves after the birth of their children.

Careline customers subscribed to a service that provided them with a dedicated phone line that was connected with a state-of-the-art call center populated by childcare experts that included mothers, grandmothers, and even nurses, teachers, and on-call physicians. The service also included a remote button that could be left in the baby's bedroom. When the remote button was pressed, it would connect with the call center, and employees there would activate its speakerphone capability. This part of the service was intended to ensure that a subscriber could get help even if they could not get to a phone.

Careline was a success almost immediately, and because it was the first in its industry, it quickly became a model for competitors. Within a decade, several other personal response companies sprang up around the country. One competitor, Care Call, was founded in 1995 and quickly became famous for its hard-sell advertising approach.

At the same time that the Care Call ad was airing nationally, Careline continued its strategy of personal selling. A team of sales representatives around the country would visit the offices of gynecologists, obstetricians, and pediatricians, espousing the value of Careline for new and nervous first-time mothers. This strategy had been successful in the past, and executives at Careline believed that speaking directly to doctors added credibility to the Careline message. This might have been true, since Careline continued its modest growth while Care Call was being investigated for deceptive business practices in several states. In April 2003, Care Call went out of business.

It had never bothered Careline executives that the media constantly confused the company with Care Call, even after the latter company had been out of business for a couple of years. If the sophisticated media were unaware of the difference between Careline and Care Call, it was safe to assume the general public was also unaware. In the eyes of the Careline executives, such confusion among potential consumers might even help Careline to pick up more subscribers.

In late 2005, Careline hired Lily Cambria, its first employee devoted exclusively to protecting the Careline trademark in marketing. She would work with both internal and external communications to make sure that the Careline trademark was used properly. To get up to speed, Cambria gathered all of the information she could find relating to the Careline trademark. The history surprised her.

Careline had been founded by a young mother who was overwhelmed when she had twins and had no close family and very few friends living nearby who were mothers and might be able to offer assistance. She came up with the idea for Careline when she found herself up with a colicky baby in the middle of the night. She knew it wasn't a medical condition that required a doctor, but she found herself needing reassurance. With a 24-hour service, she could connect with advice anytime she needed it—and not feel silly for asking even the seemingly silliest questions.

At the time of its founding, Careline received a lot of praise from the media as well as parents' groups. But because the founder was a mother who was focused on the service itself, she did not understand all of the details necessary for securing the rights to her new company's name. As Cambria found out through her research, the company had never tried to register the trademark "Careline," even though it had been using the registered trademark (®) symbol for more than a decade.

Cambria also started combing through marketing materials and employee communications from the past five years. Her intent was to take an inventory of how the different materials presented the Careline brand name. As she expected, the marketing materials used the Careline brand name carefully, typically referring to the company's service as "Careline personal response service." Employee communications, however, often used the Careline brand without any kind of description; the device was referred to as "a Careline." In other words, Careline was used as a noun rather than as an adjective.

In the marketing materials, the Careline trademark was always followed by the registered trademark symbol; in the communications to employees, the Careline name often appeared without any trademark symbols.

The last piece of research Cambria conducted related to the company's press clips. She was interested in seeing how third parties presented the Careline brand. What she found was enlightening. The company's clipping service had clipped every press article relating to Careline, but also articles that mentioned personal response services and Careline competitors. In the articles that mentioned Careline specifically, reporters had generally used the name correctly. Many of the articles that talked about the industry, however, used Careline as a generic term for any personal response service.

After a few weeks, and with all of her preliminary research complete, Cambria began to make a plan for how she would proceed with her new job of protecting the Careline trademark.

Case Discussion Questions

1. There are a number of trademark issues outlined in this case. What do you see as the major ones?
2. Cambria found major differences in the way the Careline trademark was used in external and internal communications. How would you account for the differences? What would you do to ensure that internal communications used the trademark properly?
3. Imagine that you are Lily Cambria. Thinking about the results of the research you have conducted, and what you see as the major issues that need to be addressed, write a brief plan for addressing the trademark issues at Careline, Inc.

Bibliography

Brookman, A.L. 1999. *Trademark Law: Protection, Enforcement and Licensing.* Aspen, CO: Publishers Online.

Capitman, B.B. 1976. *American Trademark Designs: A Survey with 732 Marks, Logos and Corporate-Identity Symbols.* New York: Dover.

DeNeve, R. 1989. "Whatever Happened to Corporate Identity?" *Print* 43: 92–99, 157.

Diamond, S.A. 1983. "The Historical Development of Trademarks." *Trademark Reporter* 73: 222–247.

Elliott, S. 2002. "Going Big on Brown. Advertising Newsletter." *New York Times* on the Web, Feburary 19. Available at www.nytimes.com/email.

Ellison, S., A. Zimmerman, and C. Forelle. 2005. "P&G's Gillette Edge: The Playbook it Honed at Wal-Mart." *Wall Street Journal*, January 31, p. A1.

Fueroghne, D.K. 2000. *Law and Advertising: Current Legal Issues for Agencies, Advertisers and Attorneys.* Chicago: The Copy Workshop.

G. and C. Merriam Co. v. Saalfield. 198 F. 369; 1912 U.S. App. LEXIS 1642.

Goldstone, D.J., and P.J. Toren. 1998. "The Criminalization of Trademark Counterfeiting." *Connecticut Law Review* 31: 1–73.

Johnson, G. 1998. "Pepsi Blue." *Adbusters*, no. 20 (Winter): 13–14.

Kitch, E.W., and H.S. Perlman. 1998. *Intellectual Property and Unfair Competition.* New York: Foundation Press.

Kopp, S.W., and T.A. Suter. 2000. "Trademark Strategies Online: Implications for Intellectual Property Protection." *Journal of Public Policy and Marketing* 19, no. 1: 119–131.

Koten, J. 1978. "Mixing with Coke over Trademarks Always a Fizzle; Coca-Cola Adds a Little Life in Court to Those Failing to Serve the Real Thing." *Wall Street Journal,* March 9, p. 1.

Margulies, W.P. 1977. "Make the Most of Your Corporate Identity." *Harvard Business Review* (July/August): 66–74.

McCarthy, J. 1999. "Corporate, Business and Professional Trade Names and Service Marks." *McCarthy on Trademarks and Unfair Competition.* St. Paul, MN: West Group.

McClure, D.M. 1979. "Trademarks and Unfair Competition: A Critical History of Legal Thought." *Trademark Reporter* 69: 305–356.

Polaroid Corporation v. Polarad Electronics Corporation. 287 F.2d 492 (2d Circuit 1961).

Rainwater, D.T. 1966. *American Silver Manufacturers.* Hanover, NH: Everybodys Press.

Ries, A., and J. Trout. 1986. *Positioning: The Battle for Your Mind.* New York: Warner Books.

Ruston, G. 1955. "On the Origin of Trademarks." *Trademark Reporter* 45: 127–144.

Sapherstein, M.B. 1998. "The Trademark Registrability of the Harley-Davidson Roar: A Multimedia Analysis." *Intellectual Property and Technology Forum.* Available at www.bc.edu/bc_org/avp/law/st_org/iptf/articles/content/1998101101.html. Accessed April 2, 2008.

Schechter, F.I. 1927. "The Rational Basis of Trademark Protection." *Harvard Law Review* 40: 813–833.

Sivulka, J. 1998. *Soap, Sex, and Cigarettes: A Cultural History of American Advertising.* Belmont, CA: Wadsworth.

Stipp, D. 1996. "Farewell, My Logo." *Fortune*, May 27, pp. 133, 128–135.

Two Pesos, Inc. v. Taco Cabana, Inc. 505 U.S. 763; 1992 LEXIS 4533.

U.S. Congress, Federal Trademark Dilution Act. 15 USC § 1127.

———. Lanham Act. 15 USC § 1125 (c).

———. U.S. Trademark Counterfeiting Act. 15 USC § 1127.

Wright, B.C., and Potenza, J.M. 1999. "War in Cyberspace: Battling It Out on the E-commerce Front." *USA Today* 128, no. 2652, pp. 24–26.

Yale Electric Corporation v. Robertson, Commissioner of Patents, et al. 26 F.2d 972; 1928 U.S. App. Lexis 3813.

8

Copyright Law

*The Congress shall have power . . . to promote the
progress of science and useful arts, by securing for limited
times to authors and inventors the exclusive right
to their respective writings and discoveries.*
—United States Constitution, Article I, Sec. 8

Wacky Packages, a ragtag collection of parody stickers based on popular consumer brands' packages, were born during the mid-1960s after
a comic book artist working for The Topps Company found a series of
lithograph cards from the nineteenth century. The cards were die-cut in
the shape of the day's popular brands and contained advertising copy on
the back. His idea was to reproduce the cards featuring popular brands
from the twentieth century and package those with bubble gum. Some of
the men working for him did not see the value and instead saw the idea
as just a way to sell advertising to children for other companies' brands.
Instead, the artists' team proposed making the cards into parody stickers
of popular brands. As a result, a generation of children collected trading
card stickers such as *Chock Full O' Nuts and Bolts Coffee, Kook-Aid*
instant drink mix, and *Band-Ache* bandages.

While Wacky Packages are no longer available, the 2008 publication
of a coffee table book featuring a retrospective of an entire series of
the stickers provides an interesting explanation of how copyright law
differs from trademark law—and why both are equally important in the
management of an organization's visual identity.

Even though the company was using another brand's trademark in its
own, unrelated product, the company had the legal right to do so because
the Wacky Packages were parodying the trademarks, which is a fair
use exception of trademark law. Even more important, however, is the
Topps Company's legal right to claim protection of each of the Wacky
Packages designs. Copyright law protects the expression of the Wacky

Packages designs, since copyright law is intended to protect not facts or ideas, but artistic expression.

This chapter explores copyright law and how it can be used to protect an organization's visual identity, particularly in an era where consumer-created media means there is a rampant use and misuse of the elements of organizations' visual identities.

Philosophy of Copyright Law

> American ideas of freedom are bound up with a vision of information policy that counts information as social wealth owned by all. We believe we are entitled to say what we think, to think what we want, and to learn whatever we're willing to explore. Part of the information ethos in the United States is that facts and ideas cannot be owned, suppressed, censored, or regulated; they are meant to be found, studied, passed along, and freely traded in the "marketplace of ideas." (Litman 2006)

Litman sets forth an abstract view of information, specifically that information cannot be "owned." What this view does not account for, however, is the reality that information is often viewed as a commodity. Information can be expressed (e.g., created in some form) by people who deserve to profit from their work, creations, and artistic expressions. This is a pragmatic view, and one that has been recognized by the federal government since the founders penned the Constitution.

Copyright Defined

The U.S. Copyright Office defines copyright as: "a form of protection grounded in the U.S. Constitution and granted by law for original works of authorship fixed in a tangible medium of expression. Copyright covers both published and unpublished works" (U.S. Copyright Office Web site, n.d.).

The two important elements of this definition are "original work of authorship" and "fixed in a tangible medium of expression." A work is only protected by copyright law if it is original. The work does not have to be unique, good, or even meet any quality standard, but it does have to reflect at least a minimal level of intellectual effort.

To be "fixed in a tangible medium" refers to the copyrighted work's being capable of perception—either with the eyes, the ears, or with the aid of some sort of machine—or otherwise communicated for a period of time. That is, the work is not transitory. Even Web-based content, which has the ability to be updated almost constantly, is eligible for protection. Finally, a work is considered "fixed" the moment it is written, typed, drawn, or recorded.

What Will Copyright Protect?

Even if the work of an author (in some cases, an organization) is original and fixed in a tangible medium, not everything created by individuals or the communication and entertainment industries is eligible for copyright protection under the law.

The central issue surrounding copyright protection is the place on that very fine line between two constitutional principles: an author or organization's right to profit from their creations (through the sale or licensing of them), and the public's right to free speech (Lutzker 2003). Like the concept of ensuring free speech and expression, copyright protection has been embedded in federal law since the founding of the United States, but the scope of the law has required changes to keep pace with technological advances. To ensure that both the author's rights to profit from his/her creations and the public's right to free speech are protected, copyright protection is granted for only a limited time, and the law does not protect everything an author creates (Lutzker 2003). Table 8.1 provides examples of what is eligible and what is *not* eligible for copyright protection. These are not exhaustive lists, but they do provide a sense of the scope of copyright protection. Some of the items in the "ineligible" column are actually eligible for protection under trademark law, such as short phrases that act as a tagline for a product, service, or organization, and brand names of products or services.

In the context of organizational visual identity, each individual element of the identity (name, logo, tagline, color palette, etc.) might be protected by trademark law, but it is copyright law that can provide protection when the elements of the visual identity are promoted. Whether an organization issues a press release, executes an advertising campaign, or produces a short film about itself, copyright law can protect these promotional materials from use or misuse by third parties.

To Register or Not to Register a Copyright

Copyrights do not have to be explicitly registered with the U.S. Copyright Office in Washington, D.C., in order to provide protection to an author's

Table 8.1

Works Eligible and Ineligible for Copyright Protection

Eligible	Ineligible
Literary works	Ideas
Dramatic works	Procedures, methods, systems, or processes
Choreography	Concepts, mathematical principles, discoveries, or devices (unless written into a description)
Academic papers and publications	Equations
Graphic and sculptural works	Improvisational speeches or performances (unless recorded or written down)
Sound recordings	Titles
Musical works	Names of products or services
Pantomimes	Short phrases
Photographs	Lists of ingredients or contents
Films and motion pictures	Work consisting of common information (rulers, calendars, etc.)
Architectural works	Lists or tables taken from public sources

Source: U.S. Copyright Office.

work. In 1988, the United States became party to the Berne Convention for the Protection of Literary and Artistic Property, a leading international copyright treaty (Lutzker 2003). By becoming a signatory to this treaty, the U.S. has agreed that authors should not have to endure bureaucratic formalities in order to enjoy the fruits of their creations. This translates to automatic copyright protection upon creation: as soon as a work is fixed in a tangible medium, it is protected by copyright law, but there is no public notice of the copyright ownership unless the author registers it with the U.S. Copyright Office. Registration also allows the copyright owner to register the work with the U.S. Customs Service to ensure that no infringing copies are imported into the United States.

Finally, perhaps the most practical reason an author has for registering her work comes down to money. If a copyright is infringed, the author and rightful owner of the copyrighted work must register the copyright with the U.S. Copyright Office before she can file a copyright infringement suit and seek financial damages in court.

Table 8.2

Copyright Symbols

Symbol	Denotation
©	• The most widely used copyright symbol
	• Appropriate for use on most creations, including texts and advertisements
℗	• Appropriate symbol for use on a sound recording, or "phonogram"

Copyright Notice

Regardless of whether an organization or the author of a work decides to officially register its copyrights with the U.S. Copyright Office, there is a very simple way to provide public notice of a copyright claim. At a minimum, the claim of copyright should be stated on the document (or photograph or DVD, etc.) in a visible place using the appropriate copyright symbol, the year of the document's first publication, and the name of the person or organization claiming the copyright. For example:

© 2009 Susan Westcott Alessandri

or

© 2008 ABC Organization, Inc.

This type of copyright notice, since the intent is to notify would-be infringers that they need permission to reproduce the copyrighted work, should be placed in a conspicuous place on the work: at the bottom of a print ad or just after the title page in a book, on the title page of a magazine, or on the masthead of a newspaper. In video recordings, such as television advertisements, the copyright notice might appear near the bottom of the final frame of the ad. Table 8.2 provides a brief explanation of the two copyright symbols.

Who Owns a Copyright?

While individual artists, authors, and creators are the obvious owners of their works' copyrights, the issue of ownership becomes a bit murkier when two or more people are considered the creators of a work, or when an organization's employee or consultant creates a copyrightable work.

In the case of a work having more than one creator, such as a song written by a composer and a lyricist, the law states that both creators may share equally in the copyright:

> If their contributions are inseparable, then each may lay claim to the entire work and be entitled to all the benefits of ownership in that work. In that case, however, each joint owner owes a duty of accounting to the other if the work generates income. (Lutzker 2003, p. 58)

A more common occurrence, and one that happens on a daily basis inside organizations, is that copyrightable works will be created by an individual or team of individuals in their roles as organizational employees. This type of work is considered a "work for hire" because it was created in the employee's role as employee, and because the organization paid for the creation of the work while also assuming any associated economic risk. In this case of "work for hire," the organization owns the copyright.

While it may seem unfair that an employee, particularly one who creates a work that goes on to earn millions for the organization, loses the ability to also profit from that creation, Lutzker (2003) explains that "Any employee whose job is to create work becomes disenfranchised from his or her creations, but the copyright bargain is that the person is paid for that labor" (p. 59).

While it is easy to see why copyrights for employee creations are automatically "owned" by the organizations employing those individuals, there is a second type of "work for hire" situation that occurs in the gray area where consultants and agencies work. Consultants and agencies create copyrightable works *for* the organization, but since they are not employees of the organization, it is not always clear who owns the copyright. Luckily, the courts have provided a list of factors that can help to determine if a creator is considered an employee or an independent contractor, thereby helping to determine who owns the copyrighted work. Table 8.3 lists the factors that courts consider in determining the status of an employee versus a contractor, but no one of these factors is absolute proof. Rather, the weight of the factors will differ depending on the context of the copyrightable creation (Barrett 2000).

After assessing the aforementioned factors, if it is determined that the creator of the copyrightable work is considered an employee of the

Table 8.3

Factors Considered in Determination of Employee versus Independent Contractor

Factor	Favors Independent Contractor Status	Favors Employee Status
Is there a specialized skill required for the work?	Yes	No
Is organization providing the tools used to complete the work?	No	Yes
Is the creator working on the organization's property?	No	Yes
What is the duration of the creator-organization relationship?	Brief	Long
Does the organization have the right to assign additional projects to the creator?	No	Yes
Does the creator have the discretion to decide when and how long to work?	Yes	No
Is the creator paid the same way as employees?	No	Yes
Does the creator have the power to hire and pay assistants?	Yes	No
Is the work part of the organization's regular business?	No	Yes
Is the organization in business?	No	Yes
Does the creator receive employee benefits from the organization?	No	Yes
Does the organization withhold taxes from the creator?	No	Yes

organization, then copyright ownership reverts to the organization. There is another case of "work for hire," however, in which the organization can claim ownership of the copyright *only* with the express written permission of the independent contractor. This type of "work for hire" must fit into one of nine predetermined categories. These categories are listed and briefly explained in Table 8.4.

Rights Secured by Copyright

Once an organization has secured copyright protection for its creations, either through simple notice or actual copyright registration, there are a

Table 8.4

Nine Categories of Work for Hire

Type of Work	Additional Explanation of Work
Contribution to a collective work	
Part of a motion picture or other audiovisual work	
Translation	
Supplementary work	Published as a counterpart to another author's work (includes book forewords, charts, indices, etc.)
Compilation	
Instructional text	Published for regular use in a classroom setting
Test	
Answer material for a test	
Atlas	

number of protective benefits the organization can both enjoy and exploit. Table 8.5 contains a list of the major benefits conferred by copyright protection, all of which are discussed in more detail below.

Right to Control Reproduction

When an organization creates an advertisement, sound recording, or even a book, copyright law gives that organization the exclusive right to control who copies the work and how often. Reproduction rights also include controlling digital transmission of the work. For example, the Association of American Publishers, on behalf of its member textbook publishers, is pursuing legal action against college students who are illegally posting copies of textbooks online and then making them available for download without the publisher's permission (Beam 2008). The students making the books available online are blatantly infringing each of the books' copyrights, but technological innovation has begun to outpace the law.

Right to Create Adaptations

Once a work is created and protected by copyright, an organization might use that copyrighted work, or parts of it, in a subsequent work. This is

Table 8.5

Major Benefits of Copyright Protection

Copyright protection confers the right . . .

- To control reproduction of the copyrighted work
- To create adaptations of the copyrighted work
- To distribute the copyrighted work
- To public display and performance of the copyrighted work

referred to as a derivative work, which McCarthy (1995) defines as "a work which is based on a preexisting work and in which the preexisting work is changed, condensed, or embellished in some way." Derivative works might include translations, as well as television, film, and live-theatre adaptations. Other organizations might create derivative works from their advertising campaigns. These would include the text from a television or radio advertisement being used in a print advertisement (or the text from a print advertisement being used in a television or radio advertisement).

Right to Distribute the Copyrighted Work

Distribution rights include the right to choose when, if, and in what medium a work will be distributed. In a copyright context, distribution also includes the right to publish, sell, loan, or rent copies of a work. This is what makes it possible for a copyright owner to reproduce a work and then sell and distribute it to libraries, video stores, bookstores, and individuals. What distribution does *not* include is the right of the copyright owner to control what happens after the first sale of the work. The exclusive "first sale" right accounts for the existence of libraries and used bookstores. Also, once an individual owns a copyrighted work (such as a movie on DVD or a book he has purchased from a book store), he is free to share it with others for personal use.

Right to Public Display and Performance

A copyright owner retains the exclusive right to decide when and if her work will be displayed or performed. This right is reinforced on nearly every televised sporting event, and the following announcement was made during the 2007 Super Bowl:

> This telecast is copyrighted by the NFL for the private use of our audience. Any other use of this telecast or of any pictures, descriptions, or accounts of the game without the NFL's consent, is prohibited.

Some have argued that the NFL is exaggerating its claims of copyright ownership. While the NFL obviously owns the copyright in the broadcast of the game itself, critics contend it does not own the "description" and "accounts" of the game offered by others (Masnick 2007). In fact, in claiming these rights, the organization is believed to have overstepped the bounds of copyright law as well as the Digital Millennium Copyright Act, an addendum to copyright law that makes specific legal accommodations for digital creations while ensuring them full copyright protection.

In a more basic example of the right of public performance, take a moment to think about the last time you were at a restaurant to celebrate a friend or family member's birthday. The wait staff at the restaurant might have sung a birthday song, but not "Happy Birthday to You." The staff is not allowed to sing the song because it is protected by copyright and will continue to be until the year 2030 (Alessandri 2007). If a restaurant owner sought permission to sing the song publicly to his patrons, he would also have to pay the copyright owner, Warner Communications, a royalty. When the song's copyright was sold to Warner Communications in 1989, royalty estimates were projected at $1 million annually ("Sold, Happy Birthday to You" 1989). It should be noted that people are allowed to sing "Happy Birthday to You" privately in their own homes, since this is not considered a public performance.

Fair Use of Copyrighted Materials

The right to control the copying and reproduction of a copyrighted work is exclusive to the copyright owner, but it is not an absolute right. As is the case with trademarks, there are times when "fair use" of a copyrighted work is allowed under the law.

The fair-use doctrine is an exception to copyright protection in that it provides others with limited rights to use a copyrighted work without permission and without paying a royalty. The doctrine attempts to balance competing social interests of encouraging creativity by granting copyright protection while also allowing the public to benefit from the work. In the words of the Copyright Act:

The fair use of a copyrighted work, including such use by reproduction in copies or phonorecords or by any other means specified by that section, for purposes such as criticism, comment, news reporting, teaching (including multiple copies for classroom use), scholarship, or research, is not an infringement of copyright. (U.S. Copyright Office Web site)

In the context of an infringement case where the court seeks to determine what constitutes fair use, the court would weigh four factors: purpose and character of the use, the nature of the copyrighted work, the amount and substantiality of the use, and the effect of the use on the copyrighted work. Each of these factors is discussed in more detail below.

Purpose and Character of the Use

In trying to decide the purpose and character of the use of the copyrighted work, the court is basically making a value judgment about how the work was used. If the copyrighted work was used by a teacher or professor for educational purposes, or if it was used by a reporter or other media professional in the press, the court would view those uses more positively, since they are benefiting the public. A court would view a commercial or self-serving use of a copyrighted work more negatively, therefore weighing against a ruling of fair use (Zelezny 2001).

Nature of the Copyrighted Work

There are a variety of factors that a court might use to decide the nature of the use of the copyrighted work, including whether the copyrighted work had been published or unpublished at the time it was used, whether the work is fact or fiction, and whether the work was still available for purchase (versus out of print) at the time it was used. Unpublished works are thought to need more protection than published works, and factual accounts, such as news stories, are more likely to be deemed fair use. Finally, if a copyrighted work is unavailable or out of print, copying the work is more likely to be viewed as a fair use of that work (Zelezny 2001).

Amount and Substantiality of the Use

When looking at how much of a copyrighted work has been used, the court uses both quantitative and qualitative measures. For example, the court will look at what proportion of the whole work was copied. If this amount is small, the court might deem the use fair, although this is not always the case if the portion copied is small but highly important to the larger work (Zelezny 2001).

In a landmark copyright case, *Harper and Row, Publishers, Inc. v. Nation Enterprises, Inc.*, decided by the U.S. Supreme Court in 1985, *Time* magazine had arranged to publish an excerpt of President Gerald Ford's memoirs. Before *Time* could publish its piece, the *Nation* "scooped" *Time* and published a 1,200-word article that included 300–400 words directly from Ford's manuscript. In deciding the case, the Supreme Court found that *The Nation* had published a small piece of the 200,000-word unpublished manuscript, but in doing so it had published the "focal point" of the work (Zelezny 2001, p. 311).

Effect of the Use

Because part of the reason for offering copyright protection to creators is to provide a financial incentive to create, one of the factors the court will use to determine fair use is the effect of the use of the copyrighted work on its potential in the commercial market. For example, the college students who were posting college textbooks online were essentially eliminating the commercial market for the hard copies of the books.

In a related 1991 court case, several textbook publishers sued Kinko's Graphics because the print shop was copying excerpts of books, compiling them into bound course packets, and then selling them to students. Kinko's claimed its copying of the work constituted fair use, but the court, in weighing the four fair-use factors, found that Kinko's was unfairly copying the publisher's copyrighted works, partly because its copying practices in its 200 stores nationwide were taking away from the publisher's right to collect royalty fees (Zelezny 2001).

Copyright Terms

Copyright law is a complex body of law, but one that is valuable for organizations seeking protection for the expressions of their visual identity. Organizations' Web sites, advertising, jingles, and public relations campaigns are eligible for protection—rather than the individual visual identity elements (which can be protected by trademark law). Unlike trademark law, however, copyright law provides protection only for a

Table 8.6

Copyright Terms of Protection

Date Work was Published	Conditions	Copyright Term Expiration
Before 1923	None	In the public domain
1923 through 1977	Work was published without a copyright notice	In the public domain
1978 to March 1, 1989 (date Berne Convention became effective)	Work was published without notice and *without* registration within 5 years	In the public domain
1978 to March 1, 1989	Work was published without notice, but was registered within 5 years	70 years after the death of author, or if work of corporate authorship, 95 years from publication
From March 1, 1989, through 2002	Work must have been created after 1977	70 years after death of author, or if work of corporate authorship, 95 years from publication
From March 1, 1989, through 2002	Must have been created *before* 1978 and first published from March 1, 1989, through 2002	The greater of the terms specified in the previous entry or December 31, 2047
After 2002	None	70 years after death of author, or if work of corporate authorship, 95 years from publication

Source: Lolly Gasaway, "When U.S. Works Pass into the Public Domain," available at www.unc.edu/~unclng/public-d.htm; and Cornell University, "Copyright Term and the Public Domain in the United States," January 1, 2009, available at www.copyright.cornell.edu/public_domain/.

fixed duration. It was the vision of the founding fathers to reward creators, but also to ensure that artistic expressions eventually made it into the "public domain" so that the public might also benefit from them. Table 8.6 helps to explain when a work enters into the public domain.

The Berne Convention, which became effective March 1, 1989, not only changed the rules regarding when a copyrighted work is protected (upon creation), but also how long a copyrighted work is protected before it enters the public domain, which refers to information that is available to anyone to use freely (Gifis 1998). Work currently in the public domain can be used by anyone for nearly any purpose, including public perfor-

Table 8.7

Famous Creators Whose Works Are in the Public Domain

- Ann, Charlotte, and Emily Bronte
- Mark Twain
- William Shakespeare
- Jack London
- Charles Darwin
- Charles Dickens
- Lewis Carroll

mances, written work, and sound recordings. For example, all of the work of William Shakespeare is in the public domain because it was written so long ago. For that reason, schools and community theater groups are free to stage public performances of his work while also profiting from those performances. As it stands, any work created or published before 1923 is in the public domain. A sampling of famous authors whose works are in the public domain, and are thereby free to be used by the public, is listed in Table 8.7.

Proving Copyright Infringement

Because public domain works are no longer protected by copyright law, the works are available for all to use; in addition, fair use provides for use of some copyrighted materials. Aside from these two circumstances, the unauthorized use of an individual or organization's copyrighted work will likely constitute copyright infringement.

The unauthorized use of a copyrighted work gives the copyright owner the right to initiate infringement litigation. The first step, however, is for the copyright owner to seek official registration for the work with the U.S. Copyright Office. This is the only way to ensure the award of financial damages if a plaintiff is able to prove copyright infringement.

Copyright infringement encompasses infringement of any or all of the rights associated with copyright ownership described above. In an attempt to *prove* copyright infringement, there are a couple of elements the copyright owner must prove, and then two factors the courts would weigh in determining the similarity of the copyrighted work to the potentially infringing work.

After ensuring that the work was officially registered, the copyright owner must prove that she owns the copyright in the work. After satisfying these initial steps, the copyright owner must prove that the infringing work was actually copied from the original: in the case of an exact duplication, this element of the law is easy to prove. However, if the infringing work incorporates only elements of a copyrighted work, or is a partial reproduction, proving it was copied could be more difficult. In these cases, the copyright owner can try to prove copying indirectly by proving that the infringer had access to the copyrighted work and that the copied work is "substantially similar" to the copyrighted work (Zelezny 2001).

Proving substantial similarity comes down to a two-pronged test conducted by the court. The court would ask itself two questions: are the ideas of the two works substantially similar, and is the expression of the ideas substantially similar? These questions get to the heart of copyright protection: ideas are not protected under the law; the value of ideas is in their expression. What this means is that two parties may independently create similar works based on the same ideas or facts, but copying someone else's copyrighted expression of an idea would likely be viewed as infringement.

Summary

A copyright protects "original works of authorship fixed in a tangible medium of expression." While individual artists, authors, and creators are the obvious owners of their works' copyrights, the issue of ownership becomes a bit murkier when two or more people are considered to be the creators of a work, or when an organization's employee or consultant creates a copyrightable work. In cases such as this, the organization would need to determine if it owned the copyright because the work was created under a "work for hire" agreement.

Copyright ownership ensures a set of rights, including the right to control reproduction of a work, the right to create adaptations, the right to distribute the copyrighted work, and the right to control the public display and performance of the work. However, copyright ownership is not exclusive: there are certain "fair uses" of copyrighted work. While there is no hard and fast rule for what constitutes fair use, the court would look at four factors in the case of a fair-use defense against infringement: purpose and character of the use, the nature of the copyrighted work itself, the amount and substantiality of the copy, and the effect of the copy on the market for the original copyrighted work.

A copyright is not perpetual: there are different terms of protection depending upon when the work was created and how long the author lives. For a copyright owner, proving copyright infringement starts with the first step of ensuring that the work has been officially registered with the U.S. Copyright Office. In an attempt to *prove* copyright infringement, the copyright owner must show that he owns the copyright on the work and that it was copied. In the absence of an exact copy, the court might use a test to determine the "substantial similarity" to the copyrighted work.

Case Study: Kids 4 Kids Creates an Ad Campaign

Kids 4 Kids is a Boston-based nonprofit organization that matches inner-city girls with suburban girls of the same age as a way of introducing girls to diverse families, styles of living, and neighborhoods. Each month, the girls meet with their suburban counterparts for a play date or other outing, and then every month the girls in the program come together as a group to discuss their activities and other issues of concern to them.

Although Kids 4 Kids was only six years old, it had been a tremendous success, with girls "aging" out of the program and then coming back as volunteers. The organization's success was also lauded by its primary benefactor, a foundation whose founder was raised in an urban environment and then moved with his family to the suburbs and decided more understanding was needed between the two. The foundation had renewed Kids 4 Kids' operating grant for the past five years, and a secondary benefactor had provided a grant for the organization to produce an advertising campaign to build awareness of the program both in the inner city and the suburbs the program served.

A former participant-turned-volunteer at Kids 4 Kids, Lacey Johnson, worked full-time at a local advertising agency, so she offered to manage the campaign process. Johnson even got her agency to agree to produce the campaign materials pro bono. After the agency agreed to execute the actual campaign, it was able to convince the city's major newspaper and three local television stations to carry the message free of charge.

Kids 4 Kids representatives and a small team at the advertising agency set up a brainstorming session to think up advertising concepts. It was a difficult assignment, given that the "client" was a nonprofit organization that provided an intangible service rather than a product you could touch and feel. As a way of jump-starting the creative process, the ad team decided to look through magazines to get some ideas from other campaigns.

At the next brainstorming session, which Johnson missed due to illness, one advertisement stood out to several members of the team: it was a print campaign for Boston Children's Hospital that ran in national women's magazines. The ad featured two images: one picture featured a young girl of about seven hanging upside down in a tree, and alongside that was a picture of a small girl staring up a skyscraper. The hospital's message stated that children who visited the hospital "are treated and returned to good health, allowing them to enjoy all the wonders of childhood." The text went on to provide the hospital's full name, logo, and tagline. Most members of the Kids 4 Kids ad team dismissed the ad as unusable, and the members of the team promised to meet in a few days with some fresh ideas.

The art director in charge of the Kids 4 Kids campaign, Lisa Devon, really liked the hospital ad. She kept thinking about it during the week, and the reality was that she had several paying clients' campaigns to complete, so her time was at a premium. To ease her time crunch, Devon checked to see if the hospital's print campaign was available online. When she found it on the hospital's Web site, she downloaded it into her computer's design program and began to make some changes to the hospital ad's body copy.

After viewing the ad on her computer, Devon decided she liked the way the ad looked with the Kids 4 Kids logo. She deleted the text that referred to the hospital and health generally, simply using "Enjoy all the wonders of childhood" as the complete text of the ad. Although she knew a little about copyright law and knew the hospital's original ad was protected, Devon thought her changes were substantial enough to make it a "new" ad.

Devon presented the finished concept to Johnson, the Kids 4 Kids team coordinator, and an organization volunteer. Since Johnson had been absent from the meeting in which the team found the ad in the magazine, it was new to her, and she loved it. She immediately told Devon that she adored the concept and would sign off on it immediately. Devon mentioned she had gotten the idea from a magazine, obtained Johnson's sign-off, and began to prepare the ad for the media.

Several weeks later, the chairman of the board of directors of Kids 4 Kids received a cease-and-desist letter from Boston Children's Hospital. Since the board knew very little about the development of the advertising campaign, the chairman set up a meeting with Johnson. On her way to the meeting, Johnson was confused and concerned: Hadn't the board loved the ad when she presented it to them? Hadn't they encouraged her, in fact, to try and get national exposure with the ad?

Once seated in the meeting, the board was quick to question Johnson on the origin of the ad: they asked who had thought it up, who had executed the ad, and a host of other questions. Johnson was still confused, so she asked the board for an explanation. The board explained the problem in detail—and then showed Johnson the letter from Boston Children's Hospital. It seemed Kids 4 Kids was in danger of being sued for copyright infringement if it did not cease and desist using the hospital's ad for its own promotional purposes.

Case Discussion Questions

1. Why is Kids 4 Kids in danger of being sued for copyright infringement? How can Kids 4 Kids ensure that it *isn't* sued for copyright infringement?
2. Should Kids 4 Kids stop using the ad? Does Kids 4 Kids have any right to use the ad? Could it be considered a "fair use" of the hospital's copyrighted work?
3. How might Kids 4 Kids have ensured that its own ad did not infringe the copyright of the hospital's ad?

Bibliography

Alessandri, S.W. (2007). "Branding Identity and Image Stategy." In *Creative Strategy in Advertising*, 9th ed., ed. A.J. Jewler and B.L. Drewniany. Belmont, CA: Wadsworth.

Barrett, M. 2000. *Intellectual Property: Patents, Trademarks and Copyrights.* Larchmont, NY: Emanuel Publishing.

Beam, A. 2008. "A Textbook Case of Piracy." *Boston Globe*, September 9, p. Available at www.boston.com/lifestyle/articles/2008/09/09/a_textbook_case_of_piracy/. Accessed April 21, 2009.

Cornell University. 2009. Copyright Term and the Public Domain in the United States. Available at www.copyright.cornell.edu/public_domain/. Accessed February 11, 2009.

Gasaway, L.N. n.d. "When U.S. Works Pass into the Public Domain." University of North Carolina at Chapel Hill School of Law. Available at www.unc.edu/~unclng/public-d.htm. Accessed November 4, 2008.

Gifis, S.H. 1998. *Dictionary of Legal Terms.* 3rd ed. Hauppauge, NY: Barron's Educational Series, Inc.

Litman, J. 2006. *Digital Copyright.* Amherst, NY: Prometheus Books.

Lutzker, A.P. 2003. *Content Rights for Creative Professionals: Copyrights and Trademarks in a Digital Age.* Oxford: Focal Press.

Masnick, M. 2007. "DMCA Takedown for Professor Showing How Copyright Owners Exaggerate Their Rights." Available at http://techdirt.com/articles/20070214/154327.shtml. Accessed November 11, 2008.

McCarthy, J.T. 1995. *McCarthy's Desk Encyclopedia of Intellectual Property.* Washington, DC: BNA Books.

"Sold, Happy Birthday to You." 1989 *Time*, January 2, p. 88.

U.S. Copyright Office Web site. www.copyright.gov/help/faq/faq-general.html#what.

Zelezny, J.D. 2001. *Communications Law: Liberties, Restraints, and the Modern Media.* 3rd ed. Belmont, CA: Wadsworth.

Appendix

Organizational Visual Identity Checklist

The following list of items is compiled from a number of sources. It includes many items found in a variety of organizations. When undertaking an organizational visual identity audit, change, or launch, this checklist provides touchpoints to ensure that all media have been considered.

Organizational Stationery

- ❑ Letterhead
- ❑ Business cards
- ❑ Envelopes
- ❑ Organizational checks
- ❑ Stock certificates
- ❑ Invoices
- ❑ Embossing dyes

- ❑ Bill reminders
- ❑ Statements
- ❑ Purchase orders
- ❑ Contracts
- ❑ Memos
- ❑ Rubber stamps
- ❑ Grant template

- ❑ Presentation covers
- ❑ Luggage tags
- ❑ Note pads
- ❑ ID cards
- ❑ Security badges
- ❑ Corporate china
- ❑ Proposals

Digital/Electronic Displays

- ❑ Web sites
- ❑ Interactive kiosks
- ❑ CD-ROMs
- ❑ Stock ticker symbol

- ❑ News tickers
- ❑ Bulletin boards
- ❑ Online *Yellow Pages*

- ❑ Voice-mail
- ❑ Intranet
- ❑ Extranet

Transportation

- ❑ Truck cab
- ❑ Pickup or van
- ❑ Trailer body
- ❑ Shipping containers

- ❑ Business cars
- ❑ Airplanes
- ❑ Boats or ships

- ❑ Freight car
- ❑ Parking lot decals
- ❑ Bumper stickers

Packing and Shipping

- ❏ Folding cartons
- ❏ Labels
- ❏ Shipping tubes
- ❏ Tape
- ❏ Hang tags
- ❏ Mailing labels

- ❏ Gift boxes
- ❏ Cans
- ❏ Packing sheets
- ❏ Wrapping paper
- ❏ Stencils
- ❏ Shipping paper

- ❏ Decals
- ❏ Stamps
- ❏ Paper bags
- ❏ Package closures
- ❏ Meter postmark

Employee Communications

- ❏ Employee directory
- ❏ Employee newsletter

- ❏ Employee handbooks
- ❏ Internal publications

- ❏ Paychecks

Architecture and Interior Design

- ❏ Exterior signage
- ❏ Exterior entrance
- ❏ Office name plates
- ❏ Retail store signage

- ❏ Interior lobby
- ❏ Interior design
- ❏ Interior entrance

- ❏ Landscaping
- ❏ Furniture
- ❏ Showrooms

Marketing and Sales

- ❏ Sales manual
- ❏ Uniforms
- ❏ Audiovisual
- ❏ Fliers
- ❏ Banner
- ❏ Window displays
- ❏ Shopping carts
- ❏ Info request sheets
- ❏ Fact sheets
- ❏ Catalog
- ❏ Pamphlets

- ❏ Newspaper ads
- ❏ Employment ads
- ❏ Ad insertion order
- ❏ Radio scripts
- ❏ Magazine ads
- ❏ Direct mail
- ❏ Posters
- ❏ Counter displays
- ❏ Contest materials
- ❏ Sales bulletins

- ❏ *Yellow Pages* ads
- ❏ Shopping carts
- ❏ Logo sheet
- ❏ TV ads
- ❏ Print ad formats
- ❏ Creative brief
- ❏ Co-op material
- ❏ Shelf talkers
- ❏ Promotional giveaways
- ❏ Spec sheets

Public Relations Materials

- ❐ Press kit folder
- ❐ Brochures
- ❐ Customer newsletters
- ❐ Podium identifier
- ❐ Corporate flag
- ❐ Visual identity manual
- ❐ Annual report
- ❐ Quarterly report
- ❐ News release template

Apparel and Novelty Items

- ❐ Sweatshirts
- ❐ T-Shirts
- ❐ Baseball hats
- ❐ Baby clothing
- ❐ Lapel pins
- ❐ Baby toys
- ❐ Socks
- ❐ Sweatpants
- ❐ Pennants
- ❐ Shopping bags
- ❐ Notebooks
- ❐ Posters
- ❐ Tote bags

Sources

Gregory, J.R., and J.G. Wiechmann. 1999. *Marketing Corporate Image: The Company as Your Number One Product.* Chicago: NTC Business Books.

Olins, W., and E. Selame. 1993. *The Corporate Identity Audit: A Set of Objective Measurement Tools for Your Company's Image and Reputation.* Zurich, Switzerland: Strategic Direction Publishers.

Index